Student Support Materials for Edexcel AS History

Unit 2 A1

Henry VIII: Authority, nation and religion, 1509–40

Series editor: Angela Leonard

Authors: Sarah Moffatt and Adam Bloomfield

William Collins' dream of knowledge for all began with the publication of his first book in 1819. A self-educated mill worker, he not only enriched millions of lives, but also founded a flourishing publishing house. Today, staying true to this spirit, Collins books are packed with inspiration, innovation and practical expertise. They place you at the centre of a world of possibility and give you exactly what you need to explore it.

Collins. Freedom to teach

Published by Collins
An imprint of HarperCollins *Publishers*
77 – 85 Fulham Palace Road
Hammersmith
London
W6 8JB

Browse the complete Collins catalogue at
www.collinseducation.com

© HarperCollins *Publishers* Limited 2012

10 9 8 7 6 5 4 3 2 1

ISBN-13 978 0 00 745741 0

Sarah Moffatt and Adam Bloomfield assert their moral rights to be identified as the authors of this work

British Library Cataloguing in Publication Data
A Catalogue record for this publication is available from the British Library

Commissioned by Andrew Campbell
Project managed by Alexandra Riley and Shirley Wakley
Production by Simon Moore

Designed by Jouve
Edited by Caroline Low
Proofread by Maggie Rumble and Grace Glendinning
Indexed by Michael Forder
Illustrations by Ann Paganuzzi
Picture and text research by Grace Glendinning and Caroline Green Cover photo research by Caroline Green
Cover design by Angela English
Technical review by Geoffrey Stewart

Printed and bound by Printing Express Limited,
Hong Kong

Cover Acknowledgement: *The Embarkation of Henry VIII* c.1520–40, Supplied by Royal Collection Trust / © HM Queen Elizabeth II 2012

Acknowledgements

The publishers gratefully acknowledge the permission granted to reproduce the copyright material in this book. While every effort has been made to trace and contact copyright holders, where this has not been possible the publishers will be pleased to make the necessary arrangements at the first opportunity.

p 5 & 82t from J.J. Scarisbrick, *Henry VIII* © Yale University Press, 2011 and University of California Press, 1968; p 6, 31, 89 & 111 from Polydore Vergil, *Anglica Historia (1555 version), A hypertext critical edition* by Dana F. Sutton © University of Birmingham, 2010; p 15, 29b & 42 from *The King's Cardinal: The Rise and Fall of Thomas Wolsey* by Peter Gwyn, published by Pimlico. Reprinted by permission of The Random House Group Limited; p 21 from *The Reign of Henry VIII* by David Starkey, published by Vintage Books. Reprinted by permission of The Random House Group Limited and RCW Literary Agency; p 29t from J. Guy, 'Thomas Wolsey, Thomas Cromwell, and the Reform of Henrician Government', *The Reign of Henry VIII: Politics, Policy and Piety*, 1995, Macmillan Press Ltd, reproduced with permission of Palgrave Macmillan; p 40 from *An Introduction to Tudor England 1485-1603*, Angela Anderson & Tony Imperato, Hodder Education © Hodder & Stoughton, 2001; p 43 & 115b from *Tudor Britain, 1485—1603*, Lockyer R and O'Sullivan D, Pearson Education Limited © Addison Wesley Longman, Longman Advanced History, 1997; p 49 & 63 from *The English Reformation: crown power and religious change, 1485–1558*, Colin Pendrill, Pearson Education Limited © Heinemann Educational Publishers, 2000; p 51 & 78 from *The Emergence of a Nation State 1529–1660*, Alan G. R. Smith, Pearson Education Limited © Second Edition Addison Wesley Longman Limited 1997; p 57t & 57b from *A Brief History of Henry VIII: Reformer and Tyrant*, by Derek Wilson, published by Constable & Robinson. Reprinted by permission of Constable & Robinson Ltd.; p 58, 69, 73, 79, 101, 102 & 120b from G.W. Bernard, *The King's Reformation: Henry VIII and the Remaking of the English Church* © Yale University Press, 2005: 'The right of George Bernard to be identified as the author of this work has been asserted by him in accordance with the Copyright, Designs and Patents Act 1988'; p 65t from *Thomas Cromwell: The Rise and Fall of Henry VIII's Most Notorious Minister* by Robert Hutchinson, published by Phoenix 2008 © Orion Publishing Co.; p 65c from *House of Treason: The Rise and Fall of a Tudor Dynasty* by Robert Hutchinson, published by Weidenfeld & Nicolson 2009 © Orion Publishing Co.; p 67 *Tudor Rebellion*, Anthony Fletcher and Diarmaid MacCulloch © Pearson Education 1968, 2008; p 71 *English Reformations: Religion, Politics, and Society under the Tudors* by Christopher Haigh (1993), by permission of Oxford University Press; p 82b from John Schofield, *The Rise and Fall of Thomas Cromwell*, published by The History Press © John Schofield, 2008, 2011; p 115t from *New Worlds, Lost Worlds* by Susan Brigden, published by Allen Lane, The Penguin Press, 2000 © Susan Brigden; p 99, 100 & 120t *The Early Tudor*, D. Rogerson, S. Ellsmore and D. Hudson © Hodder Education, 2001.

The publisher would like to thank the following for permission to reproduce pictures in these pages (t = top, b = bottom, c = centre, l = left, r = right):

p 9 The Art Gallery Collection/Alamy; p 13 The Art Gallery Collection/Alamy; p 16 Duncan Walker/iStockphoto; p 51l pictore/iStockphoto; p 51 c ZU_09/iStockphoto; p 51r Duncan Walker/iStockphoto; p 74 INTERFOTO/Alamy; p 80l English School/WikiMedia Commons; p 80r The Art Gallery Collection/Alamy

Contents

Foreign policy: Ambitions and problems, 1509–12

Europe in 1509: Opportunities and challenges

When Henry VIII came to the throne in 1509, it was vital that he correctly identified the main players on the European stage and strengthened his position of power in relation to them.

Scotland: There was a long history of enmity between England and Scotland. The greatest threat was the Auld Alliance forged between Scotland and France during the Middle Ages, which could be revived at any time and especially in the event of war between England and France.

The Netherlands was vital to England's economy as the centre of the wool trade. It was controlled by the Austrian Hapsburgs. In 1519 it came under the authority of Charles V, King of Spain and Holy Roman Emperor.

The Holy Roman Empire was a loose confederation or collection of states under the authority of the Holy Roman Emperor, who was elected. The Emperor's authority in this region fluctuated. He could also claim a traditional authority over Italy, which clashed with French ambition in northern Italy.

France was England's traditional enemy. Henry was crowned King of England and France in 1509, a claim first made by Edward III in 1337. Henry V was acknowledged as heir to the French throne after Agincourt in 1415 and the subsequent Treaty of Troyes in 1520, although his death prevented the claim being realised. Henry's desire to re-conquer France would be hampered by the size and wealth of the country, which far exceeded that of England, and by its alliance with Scotland.

Spain was newly unified under Ferdinand of Aragon and Isabella of Castile. It offered the best chance of an alliance with England, and was strategically well placed since it would enable France to be attacked in a pincer movement with an invasion from the north (England) and the south (Spain).

Italy was made up of a number of independent states. The Holy Roman Emperor claimed a traditional authority over them, while the Pope asserted his own claims and obstructed others who tried to intervene in Italian affairs. Both the French and Spanish monarchs had ambitions in Italy. For Henry, this presented both an opportunity to achieve allies against Italy and the threat that other nations' successes there might eclipse his own achievements in Europe.

Europe in the early 16th century

Henry's foreign policy aims

In 1509, Henry's most important foreign policy aim was glory through an adventurous policy of conquests. He wanted to follow in the footsteps of Henry V, who had conquered parts of France in the 15th century and had been acknowledged as heir to King Charles of France (although Henry died before he could inherit the throne).

However, Henry required an ally in Europe who would support his aims and assist in his attack on France. The obvious choice was Spain:

- his father Henry VII had forged an alliance with Spain
- the Spanish princess Catherine of Aragon had married his brother Arthur, and was now resident in England as his widow.

Henry also needed to ensure that the Scottish border with England was effectively controlled, to prevent any threat to his realm while he was fighting in France.

The initial quest and its failure, 1509–12

Henry was eager to embark on his war of conquest immediately. In 1509, he married Catherine of Aragon and thus secured the Spanish alliance.

However, his plans for foreign glory did not succeed. One of the reasons for this was the attitude of Henry's chief advisers, Archbishop Warham and Bishop Fox, who opposed war. In 1510, they manipulated Henry so that he agreed to extend the truce with France that had been negotiated by his father Henry VII. Henry was determined that this would not happen again.

The role of Ferdinand of Spain

In 1512, as a member of the Holy League, Henry launched an attack on Guienne in south-west France with the expectation that he would be supported by his ally, Ferdinand of Spain. However, Ferdinand was merely using Henry as a distraction to the French while he seized Navarre. Once he had accomplished this, Ferdinand made peace with Louis XII of France and Henry was forced to return to England with nothing to show for his efforts and expense.

The extract below comments on Henry's first war.

> **Source 1**
> (From J.J. Scarisbrick, *Henry VIII*, published by Eyre Methuen 1968)
>
> The campaign was a wretched failure. It is clear that Ferdinand was never interested in winning anything for his son-in-law and had always intended to use the English troops to cover the seizure by his own army of the independent kingdom of Navarre, upon which he had ancient predatory designs. Ferdinand, having acquired what he wanted, lost interest in the war.

Examiners' notes

Foreign policy was not a term that was generally in use in the 16th century, but we use it to discuss England's relations with her neighbours. A more correct term would be diplomacy. You can use either term on your exam paper.

Essential notes

The role of the Papacy in the 16th century differed considerably from its role today. The Pope was the spiritual head of Western Europe and arguably exercised total power over religious doctrine and the Church's structure and functions. He was also a significant secular power with control over significant lands in Italy. His interests therefore extended well beyond religious matters and he played a key role in foreign policy.

Essential notes

The Holy League was a loose alliance composed of the Pope, Ferdinand, the Venetians and the Swiss. It was directed against French ambitions in Italy.

Examiners' notes

In Source 1, Scarisbrick is offering his opinion on the campaign. He argues that Henry was deceived from the outset about Ferdinand's intentions. The use of the term 'wretched failure' sums up his view that absolutely nothing was achieved.

War and victory in France and Scotland, 1513–14

Henry's overriding ambition was to conquer France and claim its throne. He planned a new campaign for the fighting season in 1513.

The Battle of the Spurs, 1513

Henry was determined that his ambitions would not be undermined by unreliable allies or reluctant ministers. To this end, he made careful preparations:

- He would lead the English army himself and carry out his own campaign without relying on his allies, Ferdinand of Spain and Maximilian, the Holy Roman Emperor.
- He placed the task of supplying the army in the care of the rising star in his government, Thomas Wolsey, a man described as a 'tireless worker and natural bureaucrat' (Colin Pendrill).

The campaign began but Henry was unable to draw the French into battle. However, his troops did succeed in taking the towns of Thérouanne and Tournai, thereby fulfilling Henry's desire for glory and prestige.

From the king's point of view, though, the most significant achievement was the so-called Battle of the Spurs. Henry's troops unexpectedly came upon French cavalry who were trying to supply the people of the besieged town of Thérouanne. The French did not want to engage at that point and so they hastily retreated. This event was heralded in English propaganda as a great victory.

The campaign season in 1513 thus ended to Henry's great satisfaction. Under the terms of the peace treaty signed in August 1514:

- Henry kept the towns of Thérouanne and Tournai
- the French King Louis XII married Henry's sister Mary.

The Battle of Flodden, September 1513

Not unexpectedly, the king's absence in France provided the opportunity for the Scots to rise up and cross the English border. Source 2 details the nature of the threat.

> **Source 2**
> (From Polydore Vergil, *History of England*, published 1555)
>
> Just as King Henry had raised an Army and was about to leave for France, he learned from his money-men that the inhabitants of Yorkshire and County Durham were refusing to pay the newly-imposed head-tax, because they always hated that form of tax more than anything else. The Privy Council chose to spare them the tax, because they did not want the king to be called harsh when he was striving to maintain his subjects' loyalty. More importantly, they were suspicious of the intentions of James, King of the Scots, and feared that unless this rising was quickly dealt with, it would give him the hope of undertaking something against King Henry in his absence.

Vergil's account demonstrates the seriousness of the Scottish threat. The need to abandon the tax imposed on the northern population of England indicates a genuine fear that it might lead the Scots to invade.

Furthermore, the Privy Council was right to suspect James IV:

- he had renewed the Auld Alliance with Louis XII in November 1512
- he had begun to raise the largest army in Scottish history (30 000 men).

Henry had left Catherine as regent in his absence and the Earl of Surrey in control of the smaller army of between 15 000 and 20 000 men that remained in England. When James IV crossed the border into Northumberland, Surrey was ready to meet him. The result was a crushing defeat for the Scots:

- James was killed
- nine earls, fourteen lords of parliament and several Highland chiefs died
- a third of the Scottish army (10 000 men) lost their lives.

Catherine was able to congratulate Henry on his own victory and send him the coat of the King of Scotland to mark her own. Indeed, in military terms her victory was the more significant.

The significance of Henry's victories

The year 1513 marked the highpoint of Henry's military successes:

- He had achieved glory by conquest and demonstrated that England was a force to be reckoned with in Europe.
- Mary Tudor's marriage to Louis XII secured the peace with France, for the time being at least.
- The Scottish border was secured for the next two decades: Henry's sister Margaret was left as regent for her infant son.

Thomas Wolsey's success in supplying the English army confirmed his position as Henry's most trusted adviser, and Henry was now content to place the business of government in his hands. For the next decade, Wolsey would manage policy for Henry.

However, the victories came at significant cost and their importance was certainly exaggerated at the time:

- The campaigns exhausted the entire treasury that Henry VII had spent 20 years accumulating.
- The towns of Thérouanne and Tournai were expensive to fortify against French attack. Thérouanne had been razed to the ground by Maximilian during the campaign and required complete rebuilding.
- Thérouanne and Tournai were on the French/Burgundian border and so offered a strategic advantage to Maximilian rather than Henry.

Henry was far from achieving the conquest of France that was his ultimate ambition. Despite this, he returned to England entirely satisfied with the results of his campaign.

Essential notes

The Auld Alliance (or Old Alliance in English) between France and Scotland dates from an agreement signed by Philip IV of France and John Baliol in 1295. It was continued by all subsequent French and Scottish monarchs until 1560.

Essential notes

Henry's victory in the Battle of the Spurs is often viewed by historians as being little more than propaganda and much less significant than Catherine's victory at the Battle of Flodden. However, in his 2011 biography, *Henry VIII*, David Loades argues that Henry's judgement of international opinion was correct: victory in France carried more weight than victory in Britain isles, and so he advertised it accordingly.

Essential notes

It was necessary to appoint a regent to rule in the monarch's place if the monarch was too young, was absent for extended periods or was unable to rule due to poor health.

Essential notes

As Holy Roman Emperor, Maximilian was the overlord of Burgundy. Thus the geographical position of Thérouanne and Tournai helped secure the border of his lands with France.

The early successes in diplomacy, 1518–21

Although Henry had enjoyed successful campaigns in 1513 and 1514, he would always struggle to compete with the resources available to his rivals, the kings of France and Spain. Furthermore, when the aged monarchs Louis XII, Ferdinand of Spain and the Holy Roman Emperor Maximilian died in 1515, 1516 and 1519 respectively, they were succeeded by Francis I of France and Charles V of Spain and Holy Roman Emperor. Both were young men and likely to pursue more vigorous foreign policies.

Given these obstacles, Wolsey carved out a new role for Henry in Europe, as a peacemaker. His intention was to achieve glory and prestige for his master by placing him at the centre of European diplomacy, a role that would cost considerably less than military conquest.

The Treaty of London, 1518

The universal peace established by Wolsey in the Treaty of London was his, and Henry's, greatest diplomatic success.

Pope Leo X had called upon the European powers to unite and join a crusade against the Ottoman Turks. Wolsey hijacked the Pope's efforts to establish a European truce in which England would have been merely one of a large number of signatories. He took over the plan himself and drew up a treaty of universal peace in which England played the leading role.

More than two dozen countries, including France and the Empire, signed the treaty. It was important because:

- It committed the powers to live in peace with one another.
- Any country that broke the peace risked invasion from the other signatories to the treaty.
- Each country made an individual treaty with England rather than signing a common document.
- Henry was placed at the centre of European affairs as the arbiter (judge or decision maker) of peace.

The Field of Cloth of Gold, 1520

It was never going to be easy to maintain the peace achieved through the Treaty of London. There was a long running enmity between the houses of Valois (France) and Hapsburg (Spain and Holy Roman Empire). This worsened after Charles V's election to the imperial throne.

The Treaty of London also carried the significant risk of committing England to fighting on the side of the victim, with no guarantee of being on the winning side.

Therefore, after 1518, Wolsey worked tirelessly to safeguard his treaty by organising a magnificent meeting between Henry and Francis I at the Field of Cloth of Gold just outside Calais in France.

The meeting, which lasted for a fortnight, was characterised by jousting and other sports, entertainments and magnificent feasts. It takes its name from the extravagant tents that were built by both sides, sown with real gold thread, as shown in the painting below.

Henry VIII arriving at the Field of Cloth of Gold, painted by Hans Holbein

How effective was the meeting at the Field of Cloth of Gold?

Effective	Ineffective
Henry achieved international glory: the English displays were generally agreed to have outdone those of the French. Although it cost a year's income, it was considerably cheaper than war.	No agreements of any sort were signed. Charles V was not invited. England appeared to be siding with France rather than remaining impartial as the international arbiter of peace. Henry was defeated in an impromptu wrestling match with Francis I. Although this was hardly internationally significant, Henry felt humiliated and his feelings of enmity towards France increased.

Defender of the Faith, 1521

The final gain that brought international recognition and prestige to Henry VIII was the award of the title Defender of the Faith from Pope Leo X. This recognised Henry's defence of the Catholic faith in the pamphlet *Assertio septum sacramentorum adversus Martinum Lutherum* (In defence of the Seven Sacraments). Henry strongly defended papal supremacy in his pamphlet. It was Henry's response to the growing reform movement in the Germanic lands following Martin Luther's criticisms of the doctrine and structure of the Catholic Church.

Essential notes

The Papacy owned and controlled the lands in central Italy known as the Papal States, but effectively laid claim to rule the whole of Italy. This meant that Pope Leo opposed any ruler who interfered in Italian affairs. However, by encouraging Charles V to intervene, Leo was in fact assisting a far more powerful rival to develop his claims in Italy.

The Hapsburg–Valois conflict: Opportunities and failures, 1521–25

Reasons for the conflict: Relations between France, Spain and the Empire

The Treaty of London established a fragile peace, and by 1521 it had broken down. The main reason was the historic Valois–Hapsburg rivalry that resulted in war between Francis I and Charles V in 1521:

- Charles V won the imperial election in 1519 – an election in which both Francis I and Henry VIII competed and lost.
- Charles was King of Spain, Holy Roman Emperor, Duke of Burgundy and Count of Flanders – so his lands surrounded France (see map).
- Both Charles and Francis had territorial ambitions in northern Italy.
- Pope Leo encouraged Charles V to drive back French incursions into Italy.
- Francis invaded Luxemburg (imperial territory) in April 1521.

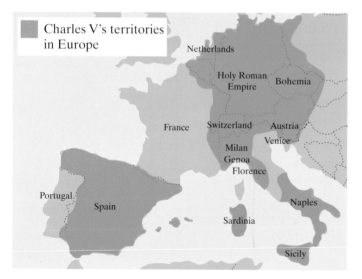

The extent of Charles V's territories

Alliance with the Emperor: The Treaty of Bruges, 1521

It was clear that the Treaty of London could not be maintained, and that Henry would be forced to make a choice between Francis I and Charles V. Charles was determined to secure an alliance with England, and Henry's personal preferences and those of his court worked in Charles' favour:

- The prevailing sentiment in the English court was one of francophobia (hatred of the French).
- Catherine of Aragon urged Henry to support her nephew, Charles.
- The merchant class depended on the textile trade with the Netherlands, which was an imperial territory, so they favoured an alliance with Charles.

As a result of these pressures, Wolsey travelled to Bruges in 1521. In August, he signed a secret alliance with the Emperor on the following terms:

- Henry and Charles would declare war on France if Francis refused to make peace.
- Charles would compensate Henry for the pensions from France (see pages 8 and 11) that he would forfeit during the war.

- The treaty would be kept secret until the French had paid the next instalment of the pension.
- Charles was betrothed to Mary (Henry's daughter).

The Second French War, 1522–23

The Treaty of Bruges kept England at the centre of European affairs, but it came with a high risk of conflict. Indeed, it was not long before war broke out between Charles and Francis over Milan. Under the terms of the treaty, Henry declared war on France in May 1522.

The war proved to be just as disastrous for England as the campaign in 1512 had been:

- Henry was let down by Charles V, who focused all his attention on recovering Milan.
- The Duke of Bourbon failed to bring the support he had promised for the march on Paris.
- The English troops, led by the Duke of Suffolk, became bogged down in the mud and returned to England with nothing to show for their efforts.

The Battle of Pavia, 1525

Although financial pressures meant that Henry was obliged to withdraw from an active role in the conflict, Charles V continued to fight. Then, in February 1525, Charles achieved a resounding victory over Francis at Pavia, outside Milan, which resulted in the capture of the French king.

Henry immediately saw the opportunity to fulfil his keenest ambition, and he sent Wolsey to make the following offer to Charles:

- Henry and Charles should immediately invade France.
- France should be divided between Charles, Henry and the Duke of Bourbon.
- Henry would assume the title 'King of France'.

The Amicable Grant and its failure

In order to take advantage of the opportunities arising from the capture of Francis, money had to be raised to fund a new campaign in France. However, the taxes imposed to pay for the 1522–23 campaign were still being collected, so it was not possible to request any more money from parliament.

To cover the costs of war, Wolsey therefore sent out commissioners to collect a so-called Amicable Grant. This was essentially a forced loan that was levied on one-third of the incomes of the clergy and laity. The levy met with resistance in London, Kent and East Anglia, so had to be abandoned.

At the same time, news came back from the continent that Charles had rejected Henry's proposal – he had little to gain by swapping one powerful neighbour for another.

In this way, Henry's dream of glory came to an abrupt end, and Wolsey was blamed.

Essential notes

The French king had started paying a pension to England in 1475. This was an annual payment of 10 000 crowns made in return for the King of England renouncing his claim to the French throne. It was stopped during Henry's first French war and increased after the return of Tournai to French hands in 1518, during the negotiations for the Treaty of London. It benefited Henry because Tournai cost £40 000 a year to maintain.

Essential notes

The Duke of Bourbon was one of the greatest noblemen in France. He was in dispute with Francis and in 1522 defected to support the Emperor. The war on France was to be a three-pronged attack by Charles, Henry and Bourbon. England paid vast sums of money to Bourbon to fund his campaign.

Examiners' notes

The failure of the Amicable Grant is often blamed for Henry's inability to take the French crown in 1525. However, you should not forget that the diplomatic mission was also a failure. Charles' rejection of Henry's proposal meant that, even if the Amicable Grant had raised the necessary money, it is unlikely that Henry would have been able to conquer France on his own.

Alliance with France and its failure, 1525–29

By 1525, it was clear to Henry that Charles V was the most powerful of the European monarchs. The size of his empire and therefore the resources that he had at his command far outstripped those of England. In addition, Charles had not demonstrated loyalty to England:

- He refused to accept Henry's plan to divide and conquer France after Pavia, and released Francis in return for promises of good behaviour and hostages.
- In 1526, Charles married Isabella of Portugal, thereby abandoning his promise in the Treaty of Bruges to marry Princess Mary.

For these reasons, the period 1525–29 saw a complete change in the direction of English foreign policy that historians refer to as a 'diplomatic revolution'. Henry abandoned the traditional alliance with Spain and the Empire, and pursued a policy of alliance with France. This provided him with new opportunities to secure gains in Europe at Charles' expense.

However, the policy was not successful and by 1529 England had been sidelined in European affairs.

The treaties of More and Westminster

In 1525, Wolsey began negotiations with France that resulted in the following agreements:

Treaty of More, 1525	Treaty of Westminster, 1527
Henry gave up his claims to France. Henry would receive an annual pension of £20000 from France.	England would enter a full alliance with France. Either Francis I or his son would marry Princess Mary.

The direction of foreign policy was not a complete change. Henry still had two clear aims:

- he should achieve prestige
- England should be at the centre of European affairs.

Negotiations with the League of Cognac

In 1526, Wolsey entered negotiations with the League of Cognac. The League intended to put pressure on Charles V to enter into discussions to cease fighting, especially with regard to his claims in Milan. However, the League insisted that the agreement be signed in Cognac and not England, so Henry, refusing to be pushed to the sidelines, would not sign.

Henry entered the League the following year, when he signed the Treaty of Westminster with France. This could be regarded as a problem for Henry. In order to acquire allies in Europe he was actually being dragged into a conflict in which he had little interest.

The Sack of Rome, 1527

In May 1527, Charles' mercenaries, who had not been paid for their services in his wars, entered Rome and began a week-long orgy of violence in which they attacked churches, shrines and monasteries. The Pope withdrew to Sant' Angelo and did not dare leave for the next six months for fear of the Lutheran soldiers, who had slaughtered the majority of his guards.

Charles V hired German Lutherans (see page 32) as mercenaries (paid soldiers) in his army. The Sack of Rome reflected their anger at not being paid but was also a religious statement about their rejection of papal authority and Catholic teaching.

A contemporary view of the Sack of Rome

Charles V may have been somewhat embarrassed by the actions of his troops, over whom he seemed to have only partial control. However, historian Peter Gwyn argues that Charles must bear some responsibility because their actions were a very direct response to Charles' demand that he meet with the Pope to begin negotiations with him over the various disputes in Italy.

The consequences of the Sack of Rome for Henry VIII

The Sack of Rome was a disaster for Henry and Wolsey. Henry's decision to ally with France instead of with the Holy Roman Empire was clearly a failure for Henry's foreign policy. It also had far reaching consequences for his domestic policy:

- Charles V, instead of being weakened by the pressure piled upon him, had now taken control of the papal heartland.

- Henry needed the support of the Pope to annul his marriage to Catherine of Aragon. This could not be achieved while Pope Clement was in the hands of the Emperor, Catherine's nephew.

- The presence of imperial troops in the Papal States meant that Clement could not act against Charles V.

The Treaty of Amiens, 1527, and its consequences

Wolsey continued to follow the anti-Hapsburg policy, and the pro-French policy developed into a full alliance in the Treaty of Amiens:

- England and France declared war on Charles V in 1528.

- England agreed to pay for the French attack.

- England suspended trade with the Netherlands to place economic pressure on Charles V.

However, the policy was not a success as a protest by English cloth workers against the trade ban forced Wolsey to abandon this policy and France was once again defeated by Charles V.

The victory of Charles V: The Treaty of Cambrai, 1529

Charles defeated Francis at Landrino in June 1528. For Francis, there was no alternative but to agree terms with the Emperor. In the Peace of Cambrai, Charles', control of Italy was confirmed.

Essential notes

Although the Pope was a major secular power in Italy, he was militarily weak and vulnerable to attack, as shown by his capture in 1527. Yet, as spiritual leader of the Christian world he wielded enormous authority. Thus, Henry could not take advantage of the Pope's weaknesses as he might have done for a secular ruler, and he needed his spiritual authority to obtain an annulment. Ironically, it may have been the Pope's secular weakness that prevented him from ruling in Henry's favour.

Essential notes

The Treaty of Cambrai marks the clear failure of Henry and Wolsey's policy. The English delegates were not even invited to the negotiations and had no influence over the terms of the treaty. Henry was not regarded as an equal with Charles V and Francis I. His policy to achieve glory and prestige was now in ruins.

Essential notes

Note that Henry's diplomatic aims changed over time from a desire to win glory, to a need (from 1527) to use diplomacy in order to achieve his annulment.

The location of the Battle of Flodden, on the Scottish–English border

How effective was Henry VIII's foreign policy, 1509–29?

Foreign policy aims

It is important to assess the effectiveness of Henry's foreign policy and the extent of his achievements in light of his and Wolsey's aims.

An examination of the aims suggests that there was little difference between those of Henry and Wolsey. Some commentators have accused Wolsey of putting his own interests above those of the king, but Henry's wishes were at the centre of Wolsey's policy. Where possible, Wolsey used diplomacy as a cheaper option than war, but this did not stop him working tirelessly to supply the money for the 1522 war.

Henry's aims	Wolsey's aims
To achieve glory by military conquest	To serve Henry's wishes
To conquer France	To place England at the heart of European affairs
To secure the Scottish border	
To establish a reliable alliance against France	To achieve glory and prestige at an affordable cost: peacemaking rather than war

To conclude that Henry achieved his aims, there would need to be clear evidence of military successes, particularly against France.

The achievement of military glory
Securing the Scottish border

The victory achieved at Flodden in 1513 secured England's northern border for two decades. Initially, Margaret Tudor was regent for her infant son. Control later passed to the Duke of Albany, but although he attempted an attack on the border in 1521, he was unable to persuade the Scottish lords to support him and the campaign ended with a truce.

Henry was not to face a serious Scottish problem until the 1540s.

The evidence presented here clearly supports the claim that Henry succeeded in his foreign policy. The defeat of the Scots not only allowed Henry to claim an important military victory, it also fulfilled another key aim – breaking the Auld Alliance between Scotland and France. This weakened France and allowed Henry to pursue his ambitions there free from the fear that he was vulnerable to an attack on his northern border.

Territorial gains in France

In the First French War of 1513, Henry defeated France in the Battle of the Spurs and took possession of the towns of Tournai and Thérouanne.

These territorial gains were a far cry from Henry's aim to conquer France, but they did satisfy his immediate need for a military victory there. They also ensured that England was seen as a force to be reckoned with in Europe, although he later exchanged the territories for a pension.

Diplomatic achievements

Some historians claim that the most significant achievement in these years was the diplomatic effort that secured European peace. Certainly, between 1518 and 1521, Wolsey placed England at the centre of European affairs with the Treaty of London and the spectacular displays at the Field of Cloth of Gold. This served Henry's purpose of achieving glory and prestige, and satisfied Wolsey's aim to keep the foreign policy affordable.

Source 3
(From Peter Gwyn, *The King's Cardinal: The Rise and Fall of Thomas Wolsey*, published by Pimlico 1990)

Where others had failed to bring about peace England had succeeded. The treaty had been signed in London with the greatest possible publicity, while England's pivotal position was built into it by the fact that the adherents only signed an agreement with England, not with each other. Henry and Wolsey as the peacemakers of Europe! It was an exciting and honourable role, and for the next three years they played it with the utmost panache.

Examiners' notes

Source 3 clearly expresses the opinion that the Treaty of London was a great success, fulfilling Henry's desire for glory by achieving a 'pivotal position' for England in Europe. Yet a hint of the limitations to the success can also be found in the phrase 'for the next three years'. You can draw the implication from this that neither the treaty nor the prestige was destined to last.

A balance sheet of successes and failures

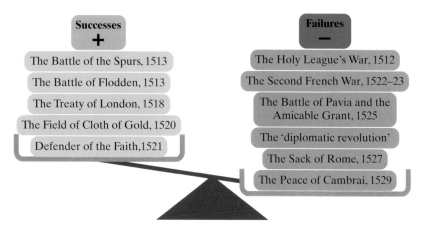

Successes **+**	Failures **—**
The Battle of the Spurs, 1513	The Holy League's War, 1512
The Battle of Flodden, 1513	The Second French War, 1522–23
The Treaty of London, 1518	The Battle of Pavia and the Amicable Grant, 1525
The Field of Cloth of Gold, 1520	The 'diplomatic revolution'
Defender of the Faith, 1521	The Sack of Rome, 1527
	The Peace of Cambrai, 1529

Weighing up Henry VIII's successes and failures

The balance sheet shows that Henry's policy was most successful between 1513 and 1521. After that time, England ceased to play a key role in Europe. By 1529, the military might of Charles V, and Henry and Wolsey's decision to abandon the Spanish alliance and ally with France, had left England on the margins of power.

Examiners' notes

The balance sheet lists the successes and failures of Henry's foreign policy between 1509 and 1529. In order to be able to use this information, it is essential that you know the events in detail, so that you are able to explain why an event was a success or failure for Henry's foreign policy. To develop your analysis, you need to move beyond categorisation into success or failure and consider how far Henry's foreign policy succeeded or failed.

Thomas Wolsey

Essential notes

Some contemporaries accused Wolsey of running foreign policy himself. Giustiniani, the Venetian ambassador, claimed that Wolsey ruled 'both King and the entire kingdom', and Polydore Vergil claimed that he 'carried on all business at his own will'. However, historians such as J.J. Scarisbrick and Peter Gwyn see Henry as the driving force behind the foreign policy. This is clearly evident in the Second French War that Henry demanded but which Wolsey would rather have avoided due to the expense.

The factors that helped Henry in pursuing his ambitions

The role of Thomas Wolsey

It is unlikely that Henry would have achieved so much if it had not been for the central role played by Thomas Wolsey. Wolsey had risen quickly in Henry's court, and by 1514 he was overseeing foreign policy for the king.

There are four key reasons why Wolsey became indispensable to Henry in foreign policy, as described below.

Pursuing the king's aims

Wolsey understood the king's aims and was tireless in pursuing them. He was also aware of the realities of English finances and sought, where he could, to fulfil Henry's wishes at the lowest cost.

Diplomatic skills

Wolsey possessed great diplomatic skills and the ability to use situations to his own and Henry's advantage. For example, he was able to turn Pope Leo X's plans for a European peace into the Treaty of London, which put Henry at the centre of European diplomacy.

Financing the wars

Henry could not go to war unless he had the necessary funds, and wars were very expensive. When Henry demanded war in 1522, Wolsey raised £200 000 through parliamentary tax. This was the largest sum that had ever been raised for a war, and it reflects the great effort that Wolsey made to argue the case for additional funds in parliament.

Supplies

One of the most difficult problems of a war was supplying troops fighting abroad. The more distant the troops were from England, the more likely they were to succumb to disease brought on by lack of food.

In 1513, Wolsey took charge of the supply routes to France and made sure that Henry's 12 000 troops were supplied with the food and weapons they needed to fight the campaign.

Wolsey did benefit from his efforts on Henry's behalf:

- In 1514, he was made Bishop of Lincoln and Archbishop of York.

- In 1515, Henry appointed him Lord Chancellor and the Pope made him a cardinal.

- In 1518, the Pope made him a Papal Legate.

These roles not only brought Wolsey riches; they also gave him the authority and reputation to conduct negotiations in Henry's name. Therefore, the relationship that developed between Wolsey and Henry was mutually beneficial.

The Hapsburg–Valois rivalry: Opportunities

Henry was able to derive considerable benefits from the Hapsburg–Valois rivalry:

- In the early years of his reign, the rivalry assisted him in forging an alliance with Ferdinand of Spain and the Holy Roman Emperor Maximilian. This was possible because France was the common enemy.

- In 1511, as a member of the Holy League, England took its place at the heart of European diplomacy. This met with Henry's desire to enhance his own prestige.

- In the First French War of 1513, Henry benefited from Maximilian's siege of Thérouanne: England received the town in the peace treaty.

- In 1521, Henry was able to use the Hapsburg–Valois rivalry to forge an alliance with Charles V at Bruges. He saw the opportunity of working with a much more powerful ally as a way to achieve his desire to conquer France. The outcome did not meet his expectations when the English troops were effectively abandoned by Charles V and the Duke of Bourbon, who were pursuing their own goals. However, this does not negate the point that the opportunity presented itself and Henry chose to embrace it.

- Henry and Wolsey were able to initiate the 'diplomatic revolution' in 1525 because Francis I wanted an ally against Charles V.

- The Treaty of Amiens in 1527 provided for the French to fight Charles V on behalf of the English. This offered Henry the opportunity to achieve a share of glory at a much reduced cost, which reflected the limited resources that England possessed.

Scotland: James V's minority

One of the most significant threats to Henry's chances of success abroad was the Auld Alliance between France and Scotland. This problem was solved in 1515 when, as a result of the Battle of Flodden, James IV died leaving his infant son on the throne. This weakened the Scottish monarchy for the next two decades:

- The initial regency of Margaret Tudor, Henry's sister, meant that the northern border was secure.

- The later regency of the Duke of Albany was subject to factional disputes and therefore not strong enough to challenge Henry.

In 1522, while Henry was occupied with the Second French War, Albany sent 5000 troops across the border and laid siege to Wark Castle in Northumberland. The castle was vigorously defended, and when the Earl of Surrey led troops to relieve it, the Scots quickly retreated.

While James V was a minor, therefore, the Scots had to be content with border raids alone.

The factors that hindered Henry in pursuing his ambitions

There were a range of factors that made it very difficult for Henry to fulfil his ambitions of conquering France and achieving glory and prestige.

Unreliable allies

Henry's aims meant that he needed allies, but those he allied himself with could not be trusted. They often pursued their own desires in spite of the agreements they had made with him:

- In 1512, Ferdinand of Spain used Henry's forces in Guienne as a distraction while he seized Navarre. He then abandoned his agreement with Henry and made a separate peace with the French.

- In 1513, Maximilian's troops sacked and burned down Thérouanne after it had surrendered. Henry received the town as part of the peace treaty, but it needed reconstructing and therefore cost more to maintain than it was worth.

- In 1522, the Duke of Bourbon failed to rendezvous with the troops led by Suffolk. As a result, the English troops were unable to advance on Paris. Wolsey became convinced that Bourbon was a player with words only, and refused to consider another campaign with him.

- The diplomatic revolution of 1525 resulted in an alliance with France. Francis I was not unreliable, but he was weak. Henry had chosen the wrong ally and was eventually sidelined in the 1529 Peace of Cambrai.

Limited resources

It can be argued that the fundamental reason why Henry's achievements were limited is that he lacked resources compared to his enemies.

Population

The pictogram on page 19 compares the populations of the main protagonists. You can see that the population of England was significantly smaller than those of France and the Empire. This meant that Henry could not raise an army to match those of the French king or the Emperor.

Income

The comparison of the main players' wealth explains why Henry VIII struggled to raise the revenues necessary to campaign successfully. The income that his father Henry VII had accumulated over twenty years was soon spent, and Henry had to rely on taxation to fund his wars. The costs of the wars are shown on the left.

A comparison of the diagrams reveals that the costs of the French Wars far exceeded Henry's annual income. It is no surprise, therefore, that between 1518 and 1521, Wolsey sought glory by peaceful means. Indeed, although the magnificent display at the Field of Cloth of Gold in 1520 cost an entire year's income, it was considerably cheaper than war.

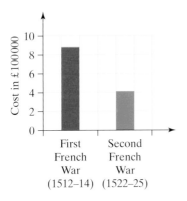

The costs of the First and Second French Wars

England	France	Hapsburg Empire	England	France	Hapsburg Empire
2.75 million	15 million	23 million	£100 000	£350 000	£560 000

The populations of England, France and the Hapsburg Empire circa 1520

The annual incomes of Henry VIII, Francis I and Charles V circa 1520

Wolsey sought to fund the 1522 campaign through parliamentary taxes and the 1525 war by the Amicable Grant. However, by 1525, funds were exhausted. Lack of money therefore played a significant role in hindering Henry's foreign policy.

The role of the Papacy

Henry did find opportunity for glory in the relationship that he forged with the Papacy:

- In 1512, he placed himself at the centre of European affairs by joining the Holy League.
- In 1518, Wolsey was able to transform Pope Leo's calls for a crusade into the Treaty of London.
- In 1521, Henry was awarded the title 'Defender of the Faith' in recognition of his defence of papal supremacy in the face of challenges to the Church led by the reformer Martin Luther.

However, after the Sack of Rome in 1527, the Pope's fear of Charles V meant that he could not satisfy Henry's desire for an annulment, even though Popes had revoked monarchs' marriages previously. This is a clear example of foreign affairs impacting on Henry's domestic policy.

Wolsey's ambitions

Historians' views of what motivated Cardinal Wolsey differ.

A.F. Pollard argued that Henry's foreign policy was undermined by Wolsey, who put his own interests before that of the king. He claimed that Wolsey desired to be Pope. David Loades concludes that Wolsey was reluctant to act, except in so far as it would bring glory to Henry. Peter Gwyn claims that Wolsey was first and foremost the servant of the king.

The evidence that Wolsey sought the papal tiara in 1521 is thin. However, Wolsey did make mistakes:

- In 1525, he insulted the Emperor in the negotiations after Pavia, and this contributed to Charles' negative response.
- The failure of the Amicable Grant was the key reason why Henry was not able to go to war in 1525.

Essential notes

Parliament granted £200 000 in taxes in 1522. This was the largest sum ever raised, but it was only a quarter of what Wolsey requested. In 1525, when Henry wanted to invade France after Charles' victory at Pavia, Wolsey tried to raise an extra-parliamentary tax, the Amicable Grant, but fierce resistance prevented this from being collected. Complaints were raised that commissioners were still collecting the 1522 tax. The protests effectively brought Henry's dreams of conquest to an abrupt end.

Essential notes

Papal annulments were granted to Louis XII in 1498 and to Margaret Tudor in 1527. R. Lockyer and D. O'Sullivan argue that the Pope would have released Henry from his marriage if it had not been for Charles V.

The structure of Henry's government

Henry VIII was 17 years old when he acceded to the throne. He inherited a system of government from his father that is outlined below.

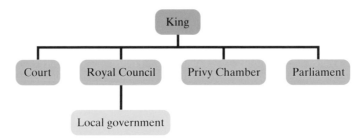

A simplified representation of royal government in the early 16th century

The king

In the 16th century, the king was the feudal overlord, military leader and the source of justice. He could make laws by proclamation when parliament was not sitting. He was seen as being anointed by God at his coronation, and he appointed the leading churchmen with papal approval.

The court

This included all the people who attended on the king. It was essentially his household. The key figures in the king's court were:

- the Lord Steward, responsible for the palace's public service area
- the Lord Chamberlain, who managed the private royal quarters.

The administration of the court was based at Westminster, but the court as a body moved with the king.

The Royal Council

The Royal Council included up to 100 members of the greater nobility, as well as Churchmen, friends and favourites appointed by the king to give him advice. It met when the king called it and would consist of those men who were available at the time. Henry was responsible for the agenda of the council, but he did not attend its meetings:

- From 1515 to 1529, the most important member of the Royal Council was the Chancellor, Thomas Wolsey.
- From 1532, it was dominated by Thomas Cromwell.

The Privy Chamber

This was arguably the most important institution in the government. It consisted of the men who were closest to Henry.

David Starkey has described the Privy Chamber as the linchpin of government: Henry's eyes and ears in the centre of government and in the counties. The Gentlemen of the Bedchamber had the most intimate contact with the king and therefore considerable influence, particularly on the distribution of patronage.

Parliament

This institution was called infrequently and usually for the purpose of taxation. The king was expected to 'live off his own' in times of peace, but taxes were raised to pay the costs of war and defence.

Parliament consisted of two houses: the Lords and the Commons:

- The Lords included nobility, bishops and abbots. Some of these men were also royal councillors. It was the more influential house.
- The Commons was elected and included county gentry (the successors of medieval knights), representatives from borough corporations and royal officials.

Local government

The king was represented in the country at large by the great noble families who had a stake in the kingdom. They in turn relied on locally appointed officials, often selected from the gentry, to ensure that the king's will and the law was implemented throughout the realm. Justices of the Peace and sheriffs were appointed to these tasks.

Henry VIII and his style of ruling

Henry VIII ruled in a very different way to his father, who had involved himself in the intricate day-to-day management of the kingdom.

He immediately endeared himself to the nobility by executing his father's royal debt collectors, Empson and Dudley, and cancelling the bonds and recognizances (a sum pledged on a bond) that they owed.

It was soon clear that Henry did not intend to be involved in routine matters of administration. This gave ambitious officials the opportunity to play a significant role in government.

Source 1 comments on the nature of Henry's style of government.

> **Source 1**
> (From David Starkey, *Reign of Henry VIII: The Personalities and Politics*, published by Vintage 2002)
>
> Many a long, lazy month was spent on horseback, as in 1526 when, as Hall noted 'because all this summer this King took his pastime in hunting...nothing happened worthy to be written of'. And even in an ordinary court day Henry was usually willing to apply himself seriously to business only in the mid-morning while he heard mass, and again late at night after supper.

However, Henry's apparent lack of interest in everyday administration did not extend to decision making and directing policy. Furthermore, opportunities for the nobility were limited by the rise of Thomas Wolsey, who by 1515 had taken charge of the business of government.

Essential notes

The members of the House of Commons were elected by substantial men of property: landed county gentry, and merchants and urban professionals such as lawyers from boroughs. Numerically, the number of voters was very small.

Essential notes

The commentator that David Starkey refers to in this extract is Edward Hall, the Tudor chronicler and Member of Parliament for Bridgenorth. Hall published *The Union of the Two Noble and Illustrate Families of Lancastre and Yorke* (commonly called Hall's Chronicle) in 1542.

Examiners' notes

The implication can be drawn from this source that royal power could ebb away in a situation where the king was liable to be distracted by amusements. In turn, the nobility could take advantage of this to progress its own powers.

Essential notes

Wolsey amassed wealth that rivalled that of the king. Indeed, he conducted so much business and acquired so many titles, that some contemporaries and historians have described him as an *alter rex* (alternative king).

Examiners' notes

Study this diagram. It shows the combination of factors that explain Wolsey's rise. In order to use these factors, you will need specific examples to demonstrate their relevance. For example, Wolsey's skill in ensuring the troops were fully supplied for the 1513 campaign enabled Henry to achieve his foreign policy successes that year, and Wolsey was subsequently rewarded with titles.

You will also need to identify implicit and explicit references to the factors in source material.

The rise of Thomas Wolsey

Thomas Wolsey was not the most likely man to be placed in charge of the king's government. However, for more than fifteen years he was the central figure in Henry's realm below the king himself.

Wolsey's background

- Wolsey came from humble stock. He was born in late 1472 or early 1473, the son of an innkeeper and butcher from Ipswich.

- He was an extremely able boy and attended Magdalen College, Oxford, from where he graduated at the age of fifteen.

- In 1507, Wolsey entered the royal household, where he became Henry VII's chaplain.

- He was soon appointed royal almoner, a position that put him in charge of the distribution of the king's charity. This gave him access to the king and hence the king's patronage.

- Between 1511 and 1515, Wolsey rose in Henry VIII's government to occupy the top position.

Wolsey's rise to power

Wolsey was able to monopolise power in the king's government through a combination of skill, good fortune and the king's patronage. Yet he was also a tireless worker, and this explains his success.

Luck
In 1515, the Duke of Norfolk was getting too old to dominate politics. Archbishop Warham resigned as Chancellor, and Bishop Fox (another key adviser) resigned in 1516. Wolsey was appointed Lord Chancellor and was able to dominate politics.

Skill
Wolsey successfully supplied the troops in the 1513 war. Later, he proved to be skillful at introducing his wishes into conversations in such a manner that the king would grant them.

Patronage
Wolsey was rewarded for the First French War with the bishoprics of Lincoln and Tournai. These were the first of many positions that the king gave him.

The reasons for Wolsey's rise to power

Lord Chancellor

This was the top political position in royal government: as Lord Chancellor, Wolsey was a member of both the Court and the Royal Council. The appointment meant that Wolsey replaced the king in terms of everyday administration of the realm, and he virtually absorbed the powers of the Council into his own person. He was also responsible for the administration of justice through the courts and for the management of the king's finances and his household.

Source 2 provides a contemporary portrait of Wolsey. It was written by George Cavendish, who was Wolsey's gentleman servant before becoming his biographer.

> **Source 2**
>
> (From George Cavendish, *Thomas Wolsey, Late Cardinal: His Life and Death*, published 1554–58)
>
> He took upon him to disburden the king of so weighty a charge and troublesome business, putting the king in comfort that he shall not need to spare any time of his pleasure from any business that should necessary happen in the council as long as he being there, having the king's authority and commandment doubted not to see all things sufficiently furnished and perfected.

Source 2 highlights the importance of Wolsey to Henry:

- Wolsey had quickly grasped that the king had little interest in the more mundane and routine business of government.

- Wolsey's inexhaustible energy and monopoly of control allowed Henry to focus on his hobbies.

This ensured Wolsey received the king's gratitude and hence rewards.

Cardinal and Papal Legate

There was a long tradition of the chief ministers of the realm coming from the Church. This was originally because education was the preserve of the Church and kings needed literate servants.

However, it also became a financial convenience because clergymen could be rewarded with Church livings that did not make demands upon the royal purse. (Cardinals, archbishops and bishops were all landholders and so were similar to princes in the state.)

Wolsey fitted into this pattern. His power and wealth relied on his positions in the state and also because, as a Cardinal, he was a 'Prince of the Church'.

Wolsey's prominence

- Wolsey was disappointed not to be appointed to the See of Canterbury. However, the position did not become vacant during his years in power.

- Wolsey was more than compensated for this when he was made Cardinal in 1515 – the highest ranking churchman in England.

- This superiority was enhanced in 1518 when Pope Leo X appointed Wolsey as *Legate a latare*, or Papal Legate.

This position of Papal Legate gave Wolsey the power to act as the Pope's representative in England. It also allowed him to appoint clerical offices and so control the patronage of the Church. As a result, Wolsey has been described as the most powerful man in England.

Examiners' notes

Henry VIII did not busy himself with routine paperwork as his father had done, but left these matters to Wolsey. This is not to say that Henry delegated the business of government to Wolsey; he was at the centre of government, deciding and directing policy.

Essential notes

The See of Canterbury refers to the office of the Archbishop and the lands and power that accompanied that office.

Although there were two archbishops in England (Canterbury and York), the Archbishop of Canterbury was the primate, having the ultimate authority over the Church in England. Archbishop Warham held this role until 1532.

Wolsey and the justice system

As Lord Chancellor, Wolsey was responsible for the justice system. Unlike his predecessors, he involved himself in the minute details of the day-to-day operation of the system and brought hundreds of cases into his own Court of Chancery to preside over them. This made him both immensely powerful and rich.

The Court of Chancery

- This court was a civil court. Therefore, it did not deal with crimes but with disputes on such matters as property, wills and trusts.
- The judgements passed in this court were based on equity or fairness. This particularly suited Wolsey because he had no legal training and so he was able to pass judgement based on what he perceived to be right.
- Wolsey heard not only the cases of the rich and powerful, but also hundreds of cases on minor issues brought before him by the poorer classes. While hearing these cases Wolsey built his reputation for justice.
- From more wealthy clients, Wolsey took lucrative bribes and gained a reputation for greed.
- The demands on Wolsey's time were great, and since he had to devote a large proportion of it to Henry's foreign policy, he established a permanent judicial committee that dealt with the cases of the poor. Nevertheless, on average Wolsey heard 540 cases a year in Chancery.

The Court of Star Chamber

This court originated in the Middle Ages as a place where the king held council meetings. It took its name from its painted ceiling, which represented a night sky. It had developed into a court of law and its importance increased under Wolsey. It represented the king's justice, with Wolsey deputising for the king himself.

Star Chamber was a criminal court. Wolsey intended to use it to tackle corruption and to make impartial judgements. Most of the cases that were heard here were brought about by litigants (persons who pursued a legal claim) and not by Wolsey.

Inevitably, a significant number were brought by the rich. When judgements went against them, Wolsey was blamed and accused of conducting a vendetta against the wealthy.

On average, Wolsey heard 120 cases in Star Chamber each year.

Was Wolsey fair in his use of justice?

Wolsey's reputation for hard work cannot be denied, but his assertion that he sought fairness above all has been questioned by some observers. They claim that Wolsey used the court system to exact revenge on and bring down his opponents.

Source 3 offers a very favourable opinion on Wolsey.

> **Source 3**
> (From a report to the Venetian government written by Giustiniani, the Venetian ambassador, in 1519)
>
> The Cardinal alone transacts as much business as all the magistrates, officers and councils of Venice, both civil and criminal. He has a reputation for being extremely just. He favours the people exceedingly, and especially the poor, hearing their cases and seeking to deal with them immediately. He also makes the lawyers plead without payment for all paupers.

The distinction that Wolsey gained for his treatment of the poor came from his intervention in matters such as enclosures. In 1517, Wolsey set up a commission to investigate the impact of enclosure on village life, and began to prosecute landlords who had not had permission to enclose.

This did address one of the great hardships afflicting the lower classes, but it was not an unqualified success – in 1523, parliament forced him to suspend his investigations and enclosures continued.

Source 4 is more critical of Wolsey's role in the justice system.

> **Source 4**
> (From Edward Hall, *The Union of the Noble Houses of Lancaster and York*, 1548)
>
> The poor men perceived that he punished the rich. They then complained without number and brought many an honest man to trouble and vexation.

This source implies that Wolsey was not concerned to be fair – clients used Wolsey's hatred of the rich to bring about false claims. Yet, it was published after Wolsey's fall, and the evidence is not sufficient to judge whether the cases brought and judgements given were indeed unjust.

Wolsey has been accused of prejudice against the rich because of his own humble origins. He was exacting in his punishment of them:

- Sir Amyas Paulet was to be kept at the Middle Temple for five years unless he forfeit (give up) all his properties.
- In 1515, the Earl of Northumberland was sent to Fleet Prison for abusing his aristocratic privileges.
- In 1516, Lord Bergavenny was accused of illegal retaining, and in 1521, of failing to report treasonable words said to him by the Duke of Buckingham. He was made to pay a £100 000 recognizance (fine) that resulted in him losing his manor at Birling in Kent.

Wolsey was in charge of dispensing the king's justice and maintaining law and order, and the cases above suggest that he did this. In this way, his work played a key role in strengthening royal power, because the king's justice was rigorously enforced and no one, not even the most powerful, could evade it.

Examiners' notes

Source 3 has many merits. Giustiniani would have had contact with Wolsey and was in a position to know about his work, although his information has probably come from Wolsey's supporters. The reference to Wolsey's treatment of the poor implies that he did not favour the rich, and compulsion on lawyers to plead cases for free would very likely have been resented.

Essential notes

Enclosure was the practice of fencing off common land so that it ceased to be available to the people but only to the landowner. It was a significant burden to the poorer classes, who used the common land to graze their livestock and to gather wood and other essential resources.

Essential notes

Retaining refers to the practice of recruiting men from the gentry and lower social classes as servants. They were placed in uniform and had a military as well as domestic role. This practice was outlawed by Henry VIII because of the danger that the nobility could use it to build private armies and challenge the authority of the monarch.

Wolsey and the strengthening of royal finances

Henry VII had left the monarchy in a stable financial position. Henry VIII's decision to pursue an adventurous foreign policy, coupled with the cost of court entertainments, meant that Wolsey had to maximise the returns from the existing system and find new sources of revenue.

The sources of Henry's income

The king could call upon the following finances:

- income from Crown lands
- customs duties granted by parliament for the duration of his reign
- feudal dues such as wardships for minors
- parliamentary taxation: fifteenths and tenths.

Income from Crown lands

This income had been falling because Henry had granted lands away from the Crown at the beginning of his reign.

Wolsey rectified this situation by pushing the Act of Resumption through parliament in 1515. This restored some of the lands and brought an improvement to Henry's financial situation.

Royal taxes: Fifteenths and tenths

It was expected that the king would be able to finance his living from his own income, but provision was made for additional money to pay for war and its associated costs. In these circumstances, Henry could request parliamentary taxes.

The standard form of taxation in England was fifteenths and tenths. These were fixed rates that were paid by towns and boroughs. They were not related to the actual wealth of those areas. Although Wolsey could request these taxes from parliament, the fixed rate meant that the yield would not be sufficient for Henry's needs.

The Subsidy

Wolsey found the solution that he needed in the introduction of the Subsidy. This was also a parliamentary tax, but it was based on an accurate assessment of taxpayers' income and was much more flexible, so that it would increase as the wealth of the taxpayer increased.

Taxation and the role of parliament

Parliament was summoned infrequently and usually for the purpose of raising taxes.

Wolsey requested taxes on the king's behalf in the parliaments of 1512–14, 1515 and 1523. The taxes were granted but not always at the levels Wolsey demanded.

In 1524, Wolsey asked for a Subsidy of four shillings in the pound, which would have provided £800 000. However, he was bitterly resisted in the Commons, and in the end a Subsidy of two shillings was granted. This did net £200 000, the largest sum ever raised by a single taxation, but it was significantly less than Wolsey had wanted and needed.

Forced loans

One reason why Wolsey had experienced difficulty in raising the Subsidy in 1523 was the forced loan that he had exacted in March and July 1522.

In order to raise finances for the Second French War, Wolsey twice despatched commissioners to assess the military and financial resources of each county. He subsequently compelled the payment of a 'loan' to the Crown. In total, Wolsey raised the sums shown in the diagram below right.

The Amicable Grant, 1525

Following Francis I's capture in the Battle of Pavia in 1525, Wolsey needed to raise funds for the king's conquest of France. To avoid the chance of another dispute in parliament, he decided to use an innovation that he termed an 'Amicable Grant'.

The Amicable Grant was called 'benevolence' by Wolsey, to give the impression that it was a gift. However, it was essentially a tax that had not been approved by parliament, and so the legal basis for its collection was very weak. It was levied on a third of the incomes of laity and clergy.

The result was a disaster: there were riots in Lavenham in Suffolk and in other parts of East Anglia and in Kent. Henry was obliged to step in and cancel the levy.

For the first time, Wolsey had failed his master. Although there were no immediate repercussions for him, this would be the first nail in Wolsey's coffin; his enemies would ensure that Henry did not forget that Wolsey had prevented him becoming King of France.

Reducing royal expenditure

One way in which Wolsey sought to improve royal finances was to reduce spending. In particular, he tackled the spiralling costs of the king's household and the lavish use of patronage:

- In 1515, an Act of Resumption was passed that revoked a number of royal grants and saved up to £10 000 a year.

- In 1519, Wolsey persuaded Henry to dismiss Gentlemen of the Privy Chamber in what has been called the expulsion of the minions.

- In 1526, in the Eltham Ordinances, Wolsey reduced the Gentlemen of the Bedchamber from twelve to six.

- Behind the scenes, as many as 2000 royal servants who were employed in lesser roles in the royal household were also removed. There was a significant saving by cutting their board and lodgings.

By these measures, royal finances were brought under control with a surplus of £107 000 a year. However, despite Wolsey's efforts, the king's ordinary income was never sufficient for his needs because of his expensive foreign policy.

Essential notes

The king had the right to demand money from his subjects without the approval of parliament in times of war. Forced loans were technically to be repaid and this was guaranteed with a receipt from the Privy Seal. However, Wolsey used parliament to convert these loans to a gift by statute, so the 1522 forced loans were never repaid.

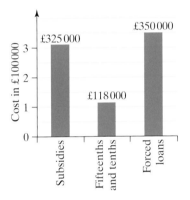

Finances raised by Wolsey

Essential notes

It has often been claimed that Wolsey was solely behind the expulsion of the minions. Yet according to David Loades, this policy was favoured by the whole royal council, who feared the influence of these young men who were so close to the king. Peter Gwyn claims that the move had more of a political than economic effect and the minions were soon restored. However, the cost cutting lower down in the household was entirely economic.

Wolsey's relationship with the king

Was Wolsey an 'alter rex'?

Wolsey has been accused by G.R. Elton of trying 'to rule as king when he was not the king', behaving as an 'alter rex', or alternate king. It is not difficult to understand how such an opinion emerged:

- Routine business was placed in Wolsey's capable hands while Henry indulged his preference for sports.
- Wolsey's palace at Hampton Court rivalled the splendour of the royal palaces, and Wolsey frequently received ambassadors there.
- Wolsey's wealth enabled him to distribute patronage.
- Wolsey's titles of Cardinal and Papal Legate elevated his rank to challenge the king.
- Unpopular decisions were blamed on Wolsey and this left the impression that he was directing and responsible for policy.

There is contemporary evidence to support this point of view:

> **Source 5**
> (From George Cavendish, *Life of Wolsey*, 1554–58)
>
> He took it upon himself to disburden the king of so weighty a charge and troublesome business, putting the king in comfort that he shall not need to spare any time of his pleasure for any business that should necessary happen in the council as long as he being there, having the king's authority and commandment doubted not to see all things sufficiently perfected.

From an initial reading, it could be thought that Wolsey monopolised power while encouraging the king to pursue his sports. However, key phrases in the extract give a different impression:

- Cavendish's emphasis that Wolsey had the 'king's authority' makes it quite clear that Wolsey could not pursue his own independent policy.
- The phrase 'business that should necessary happen in the council' suggests Cavendish is referring to routine, everyday affairs.

Wolsey was very clear on Henry's attitude and desires so could have implemented the king's wishes without constant reference to him. Where there were questions that required the king's authority, Cavendish notes:

> **Source 6**
> (From George Cavendish, *Life of Wolsey*, 1554–58)
>
> [He] would first make the king privy of all such matters before he would proceed to the finishing and determination of the same whose mind and pleasure he would fulfil and follow to the uttermost wherewith the king was wonderfully pleased.

The view of Wolsey as an 'alter rex' is challenged by John Guy:

> **Source 7**
> (From J. Guy, 'Thomas Wolsey, Thomas Cromwell, and the Reform of Henrician Government', in *The Reign of Henry VIII: Politics, Policy and Piety*, published by Palgrave Macmillan 1995)
>
> Between 1515 and 1525 it can be argued that Henry treated him more as a partner than a servant. Wolsey enjoyed a uniquely privileged access to the king. They walked arm-in-arm together and were intimate confidantes to the exclusion of others.

The opinion that Wolsey and Henry were partners is supported by Peter Gwyn, but he is quite clear that it was not a partnership of equals:

> **Source 8**
> (From Peter Gwyn, *The King's Cardinal: The Rise and Fall of Thomas Wolsey*, published by Pimlico 1992)
>
> Wolsey was Henry's leading councillor because the king trusted him to carry out his wishes, but it was Henry who was king, and Wolsey was never allowed to forget it.

A study of Wolsey's relationship with the king, therefore gives the impression that royal authority was supported rather than challenged by it. This can be supported when you examine the circumstances of Wolsey's fall. Wolsey's fall cannot be separated from his failure to satisfy the king's demands. This would not be the case if Wolsey's powers exceeded those of the king.

How far was royal power strengthened?
Wolsey strengthened rather than challenged the authority of the king:

- He took the blame for the failures of the regime such as the disastrous Amicable Grant.
- He brought the nobility under control by packing the Privy Chamber with his supporters, such as his chamberlain Sir Richard Page and the royal secretary Richard Pace. The fate of nobles like Buckingham also served as a reminder to the nobility that they were not above the law.
- He managed parliament to deliver the finances necessary for the king to pursue his foreign policy although never in sufficient amount for Henry to achieve everything he wanted.

There is little evidence that Henry's authority was weakened because of Wolsey's role. Those historians who claim Wolsey undermined Henry refer to the evidence below:

- his personal wealth, which was greater than that of the king
- his palace at Hampton Court to which ambassadors sometimes came before they went to the King's palace
- his use of gifts to impress the king and to manipulate him into agreeing with Wolsey's views.

Examiners' notes

These secondary sources are good examples of how historians express their opinions based on the contemporary sources consulted. Elton, Guy and Gwyn will all have used Cavendish in their research, but Guy and Gwyn have differed from Elton significantly in their judgements.

Essential notes

According to Gwyn, the relationship between king and minister is best understood in the way that a managing director would run a company on behalf of the chairman.

Examiners' notes

An assessment of Henry's foreign and domestic policy supports J.J. Scarisbrick's view that while Wolsey needed to be able to exercise power in order to direct policy on behalf of Henry, at the same time it was dangerous to give the impression that he was usurping power. Wolsey was allowed to pursue policies that enhanced the king's prestige and authority, but he could not form his own policy that contradicted the king. Hence, in the 1520s, Wolsey worked tirelessly to raise the finances to fight wars that destroyed the peace he established in the Treaty of London, 1518.

Essential notes

Faction refers to a group of people who sought to advance their own interests in government.

Examiners' notes

Study the diagram. This is a good example that you can use for planning a response to a question focusing on noble opposition to Wolsey. The five key factors on the diagram each played a role. You have studied them in detail on pages 22–29. Use the factors as prompts to examine the factors in more detail in your answer.

Wolsey's relationship with the nobility and parliament

An opinion that is often expressed is that Wolsey was loathed by the nobility who worked tirelessly to bring him down. In this version, Wolsey was the victim of factional intrigue.

Factional struggle: Wolsey and the nobility

Factional struggle was rife in Henry's reign, although the composition and focus of the factions changed constantly. For example, Nicholas Carew, a Gentleman of the Bedchamber, was a member of the anti-Wolsey faction in the early 1520s; by the mid 1520s, he was in the Aragonese faction, which directed its opposition more directly against the Boleyn faction than against Wolsey.

The diagram below summarises the key reasons why Wolsey was resented by the nobility and became the victim of factional opposition.

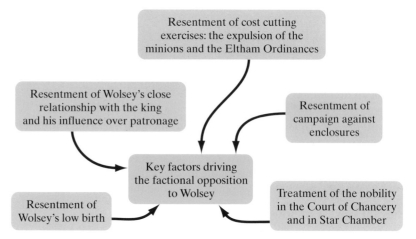

Reasons why different factions opposed Wolsey

Contemporary historian Polydore Vergil claimed that Wolsey's involvement in the arrest and execution of the Duke of Buckingham convinced the nobility that he was their enemy (see Source 9). Buckingham was a sympathiser with the White Rose Party and had a claim to the throne as a descendant of Edward III. He was therefore extremely dangerous to the king. He was found guilty of illegally retaining men and of plotting to kill the king and was executed in 1521.

Wolsey's treatment of some nobility in the courts and his campaign against enclosures confirmed suspicions that he deliberately sought to humiliate the nobility.

For his part, Wolsey was suspicious of those who had access to Henry in the Bedchamber. His cost cutting exercises (expelling the minions in 1519 and the Eltham Ordinances in 1526) also had a political benefit for Wolsey; they reduced the influence of the nobles and gentry and their sons in an area of the court that was restricted to him.

Examiners' notes

Polydore Vergil's interpretation is not accepted by historians John Guy and Peter Gwyn. They refer to the clear involvement of the king in Buckingham's arrest and trial and the fact that he was condemned by twenty peers. The nobility continued to seek favours from Wolsey after Buckingham's death.

Source 9
(From Polydore Vergil, *Anglica Historia*, 1555)

[Wolsey] burned with hatred and, thirsting for human blood, decided to encompass the downfall of Duke Edward of Buckingham, as he had already made up his mind to do. Wolsey went to the king and told him his life was in danger, accused the duke of treason, and said that evidence of this crime had now come to light. He urged him to protect himself and his family from this peril as soon as possible.

Wolsey and parliament

Wolsey is often regarded as disliking parliament, and it is sometimes claimed that this is why he called it infrequently. However, in the 16th century, the primary purpose of parliament was to raise money. So, if the king did not need money, it was not necessary to summon it, and hence it was usual for it only to be called infrequently.

Wolsey, as Archbishop of York, was a member of the House of Lords. He did not face challenges in this chamber, but there was resentment in the Commons because of his wealth, and because he represented the clergy that (as many MPs believed) abused their positions.

This was shown most obviously in the outbursts against the treatment of Richard Hunne in 1515 and in the 1529 Parliament where there was great criticism of Wolsey.

The table below shows the parliaments that sat before 1529 when Wolsey was in his ascendancy:

Date	Key issue	Details
1512–24	Finances for war	Three tenths and fifteenths were granted and the Subsidy was introduced
1515	The Hunne case	Criticism of the clergy after the murder of suspected heretic Richard Hunne
1523	Finances for war	£200 000 was raised in taxes for the Second French War

The table suggests that parliament was not a threat to Wolsey before 1529. On the occasions when he requested taxes, they were granted, although not always in the amounts desired. It was not called frequently because policy was made in the king's household. It would therefore be a mistake to see Wolsey as undermined in parliament before his fall in 1529.

Examiners' notes

Source 9 clearly argues that Wolsey was responsible for Buckingham's downfall. However, Vergil, writing after Wolsey's death, had been imprisoned by Wolsey for a short period in 1515 and so his remarks have to be treated with caution. David Starkey argues that Buckingham's execution was the result of the threat that he posed rather than a vendetta by Wolsey.

Essential notes

The 1529 Parliament was summoned in part to assist in the removal of Wolsey. This is examined in detail on pages 36–37.

Essential notes

Nevertheless, Wolsey took care not to antagonise parliament. In 1525 he had avoided calling it to raise taxes for Henry's proposed campaign after Francis I's defeat at Pavia. This implies that he believed he would face opposition to any further requests for taxation.

Wolsey and the Church

Wolsey's powers in the Church

Wolsey was not only the most important statesman in England after the king; he was also the most important churchman.

Wolsey held the following positions in the Church: Bishop of Lincoln until he became Archbishop of York in 1514; Bishop of Tournai; Abbot of St Albans; Cardinal; *Legate a latere* (Papal Legate).

The most significant of these was Papal Legate. It put Wolsey in a unique position to control the Church, including the See of Canterbury (the office of the primate).

Contemporaries and historians who have regarded Wolsey as primarily motivated by greed claim that the acquisition of the powers held by the legate were Wolsey's main motivation. As legate he was able to:

- make visitations to all dioceses
- appoint all benefices that were in the Church's patronage
- summon Church councils
- make new rules for the clergy, including monks and nuns
- claim Canterbury's authority and revenues.

There is no doubt that the position made him both powerful and wealthy. It also put him in the prime position to tackle the problems that were confronting the 16th-century Church.

Wolsey and the reform of the Church

While Wolsey has gained a reputation for tackling problems in the justice and financial system, his record in the Church is much less impressive.

There were a number of abuses in the Church that required reform:

- pluralism (holding more than one church office)
- absenteeism (failure of the bishop to live in his diocese)
- nepotism (giving a church office to a family member)
- simony (buying and selling church offices)
- sexual misconduct (clergy were supposed to remain celibate, but there were frequent cases of priests keeping a mistress)
- poor education (some parish priests could barely read, so were in no position to explain the complexities of the Bible to their parishioners).

However, there is considerable debate on the condition of the English Church in the early 16th century. How far the Church was under threat from the challenges of the Reformation is not clear. A.G. Dickens has described it as 'poorly equipped to weather the storms of the new age'; whereas E. Duffy claims that it had a 'vigorous hold over the imagination and loyalty of the people'.

Essential notes

The authority as legate was first awarded to Wolsey in 1518 in order to enable him to fulfil the Pope's desire for a crusade against the Turks, but it was renewed and awarded for his lifetime in 1524.

Essential notes

Benefices were Church offices that came with land or other forms of income.

Essential notes

It is claimed that Wolsey did not implement the reforms that were necessary to protect the Church from attack later on. John Guy argues in *Tudor England* (1988) that Wolsey's policy in the Church never extended beyond 'good intentions'.

Essential notes

The Reformation in Europe is often dated from 1517, when Martin Luther pinned his 95 Theses on a church door in Wittenberg. His criticisms soon developed into a rejection of papal authority, the special status and importance of the clergy, and key Catholic doctrines.

Key issue	Problem	Wolsey's solution
Church courts	Cases against clergy accused of committing crimes were treated more leniently than in the lay courts. This was known as the 'benefit of clergy'.	An Act of 1512 removed the benefit of clergy for serious crimes from clerics who were not in holy orders. Wolsey agreed with the king that the benefit could not apply to those who had not taken holy orders. In doing this, he preserved the benefit for clerics in orders. The abuse therefore continued.
The behaviour of the clergy	Some clergy were poorly educated and their behaviour was not fitting for men of the cloth.	Wolsey held an ecclesiastical council at York to investigate ways of improving behaviour, but nothing was implemented.
Reform of the monasteries	Some monks were living too comfortably and were too involved in worldly matters.	Wolsey visited various monasteries, closing down 30 that were not viable (they had shrunk to very low numbers). He used the money from the dissolved monasteries to build his own college, Cardinal College, at Oxford.

The evidence from the table above suggests that Wolsey did not pursue reform with vigour. By not addressing the key issues that prompted criticism, he became associated with the corruption.

Simon Fish, a supporter of reform in the Church, directed his anti-clericalism explicitly at Wolsey's protection of clerical abuses. In the source below, he claims that Wolsey used his power and wealth to subvert the laws of Christ:

> **Source 10**
> (From Simon Fish, *Supplication for the Beggars*, 1529)
>
> What law can be made so strong against them that they either with money or else with other policy will not break or set at nought? What kingdom can endure that ever gives thus and receives nothing?

Clerical abuses: Wolsey's role and attitude

It could be argued that Wolsey's own behaviour had a negative impact on the Church, so he was not best placed to deal with the complaints. Indeed, he had a vested interest in maintaining the Church's benefits at the expense of reform.

When he did intervene to restrict benefit of clergy, Wolsey was mainly concerned that the Church bowed to royal authority. There is little evidence that he used his powers to address the burning issues of the day, and this is demonstrated in the anti-clerical outbursts against him in the 1529 parliament (see page 37).

Yet Wolsey did not really behave differently to other leading churchmen in Europe. He also had the difficult task of shielding the Church from monarchical attack while assuring the king that the Church was not undermining his prerogative.

Examiners' notes

Note that Wolsey's closure of 30 monasteries and his use of the wealth gained for his own benefit set a precedent for Henry's dissolution of the monasteries in the 1530s. Wolsey had demonstrated that it was legitimate to seize Church property and use it for other purposes.

Essential notes

Wolsey was guilty of many of the abuses that promoted criticism:

- pluralism – he held several bishoprics
- absenteeism – he did not visit the seat of his archbishopric in York until he fell from power
- simony – he bought offices for his illegitimate son Thomas Winter
- sexual misconduct – he kept a mistress by whom he had two children.

How successful was Wolsey as Chancellor?

Wolsey managed Henry's government for fifteen years. His priority, according to Peter Gwyn, was always to fulfil the king's wishes. This would also allow him to maintain his own position of power.

In order to achieve this, and to ensure that affairs in the kingdom ran smoothly, Wolsey focused on the aims detailed below:

- to manage finances so that the king's policies were affordable
- to keep the nobility under control and prevent any threats to Henry
- to achieve justice for all in the legal system
- to manage parliament and the Church so they supported the king.

Finances

A balance sheet of Wolsey's financial achievements would look like this:

+	−
• New source of income (the Subsidy) was introduced and collected four times. In 1523, it raised £200 000 for war against France. This was the largest sum ever for a single tax. • Reduction of expenditure – the expulsion of the minions in 1519 and the Eltham Ordinances in 1526 cut the costs of the Bedchamber.	• In 1523, Wolsey requested £800 000 from the Subsidy but Parliament only granted £200 000, a quarter of the sum requested. • The Amicable Grant sparked such opposition in 1525 that it had to be abandoned without a penny collected. It was one reason why Henry was unable to take advantage of Francis I's defeat at Pavia. • The Eltham Ordinances alienated the nobility, whose sons often held positions in the Bedchamber.

The legal system

In 1515, Wolsey claimed that he wanted to achieve justice for all. A balance sheet of Wolsey's judicial achievements would look like this:

+	−
• 120 cases a year heard in the Court of Star Chamber, compared to an average of 12 under Henry VII. • 540 cases a year heard in the Court of Chancery, including many from those of poorer backgrounds. • Wolsey established the Court of Requests where there was no fee. • 1517 inquiry into enclosures indicates that Wolsey was addressing a key grievance for the poorer classes.	• Wolsey took bribes and personally enriched himself. • The nobility accused Wolsey of using the legal system to conduct vendettas against them. • The inquiry into enclosures was suspended in 1523 because of opposition from landowners in parliament.

Parliament

Since Wolsey did not need to call parliament unless he needed money, it did not unduly trouble him. The balance sheet for finances details the success of his requests for taxation; it suggests that, overall, his relationship with parliament was not unsuccessful.

The Church

Wolsey's aims in the Church are difficult to pinpoint because his roles were conflicting. He was expected to protect the Church against the state while at the same time ensuring that nothing diminished the powers of the king.

The balance sheet below does not reflect well on Wolsey and provides some explanation as to why he was associated with abuses in the Church:

+	−
• He increased his personal wealth and prestige. • He protected benefit of clergy from the king's and parliament's attempts to end it. • He dissolved 30 monasteries that were not viable because of low numbers.	• By maintaining benefit of the clergy Wolsey protected abuses in the Church. • He used the money from dissolved monasteries to fund the foundation of Cardinal College, Oxford. • He became associated with clerical abuses. • He admitted that royal power was superior to ecclesiastical power. • He left the Church vulnerable to attack because he had done little to introduce reforms.

Essential notes

The term anti-clerical refers to opposition to the clergy's interference in secular (non-religious) affairs.

The nobility and factions

The heart of government was in the Privy Chamber and the Royal Council. Henry wanted Wolsey to control the power of the nobility here.

+	−
• He prevented Buckingham's 'plot' to overthrow Henry. • He reduced the influence and cost of the nobility by expelling the minions and the Eltham Ordinances. • He brought the north under control by appointing the 6th Earl of Northumberland as warden of the East and Middle Marches, with the task of subduing the threat posed by Sir William Lisle.	• Wolsey was blamed for the execution of Buckingham. • He faced opposition over the Amicable Grant by the Dukes of Norfolk and Suffolk. • He was opposed over the issue of enclosures. • Some regarded him as using the legal system to pursue prejudices against nobles.

Essential notes

Sir William Lisle was the Lord of Felton, the head of an important family on the borders with Scotland. He and his son Humphrey had broken out of prison in 1527, releasing a number of other prisoners with them, and began causing chaos in the north.

Opposition from the nobility left Wolsey vulnerable to attacks when he lost the king's favour. This was of some significance in his downfall.

Wolsey's fall from power

By 1529, Wolsey was becoming overwhelmed by the failures of his policies.

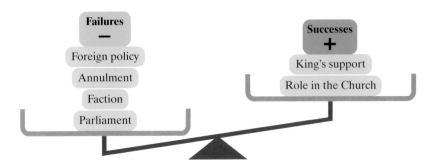

Weighing up Wolsey's successes and failures

The failure of Wolsey's foreign policy, 1525–9

- Wolsey had not delivered any foreign policy successes since 1520.

- The diplomatic revolution of 1525–27 was a failure. The alliance with France put England on the losing side in the Hapsburg–Valois struggle.

- Francis I was defeated again at Landriano in June 1529, and England was stranded on the sidelines in the Peace of Cambrai in August.

- The Sack of Rome in 1527 had made it impossible for the Pope to agree to Henry's request for an annulment. This failure caused Henry to recall Wolsey's failure over the Amicable Grant, and the king lost faith in his Chancellor.

The failure of Wolsey's strategy in Henry's annulment

The key issue by 1529 was the resolution of the 'King's Great Matter' – the annulment of Henry's marriage to Catherine. Henry had entrusted the case to Wolsey, who had assured him that he would be able to obtain the annulment. However, Wolsey's strategy completely failed:

- In 1527, he passed the case to Rome, but the Sack of Rome and the Pope's capture prevented the Pope declaring Henry's marriage invalid.

- Wolsey's attempt to be elected as acting Pope was blocked by opposition from the French cardinals.

- The court held at Blackfriars in the summer of 1529 failed when Catherine appealed and Cardinal Campeggio, who was hearing the case with Wolsey, referred the case back to Rome.

Wolsey's hold on power had depended on him satisfying the king's desires. When he could no longer do this, his downfall was inevitable.

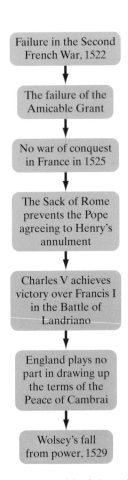

Failure in the Second French War, 1522

↓

The failure of the Amicable Grant

↓

No war of conquest in France in 1525

↓

The Sack of Rome prevents the Pope agreeing to Henry's annulment

↓

Charles V achieves victory over Francis I in the Battle of Landriano

↓

England plays no part in drawing up the terms of the Peace of Cambrai

↓

Wolsey's fall from power, 1529

Summary of the failure of Wolsey's foreign policy

The role of the nobility and factional struggle

It has been a popular claim by historians that Wolsey's downfall can be attributed to the growth of the anti-Wolsey faction. The membership of the faction included:

- the Duke of Norfolk, who opposed Wolsey's lowly origins and his influence over the king

- Anne Boleyn, Norfolk's niece and Henry's intended bride, who also opposed Wolsey because he had prevented her earlier betrothal to Henry Percy, heir to Northumberland

- Thomas Boleyn, Anne's father, who was frequently in the king's presence and seized the opportunity to improve the power and influence of himself and his family.

There is evidence to support the claim that this faction operated in 1529 to put pressure on Henry to dismiss Wolsey. Wolsey had no supporters among the other factions at court; the Aragonese faction was just as opposed to him for trying to bring about the annulment.

However, according to Peter Gwyn (*The King's Cardinal,* 1992) 'it was Henry who made Wolsey, and it was Henry who destroyed him'; the factions presented Henry with an opportunity but they could not destroy Wolsey on their own.

Wolsey's arrest and removal from office

On 9 October 1529, Wolsey was charged with praemunire, stripped of his state offices and sent to his diocese of York that he had never visited. He hoped to restore himself to the king's favour and sent many letters to his subordinate, Thomas Cromwell, begging him to intercede with the king. Although Cromwell initially defended Wolsey in parliament valiantly, he was unable to satisfy Wolsey's requests to rehabilitate his old master and retrieve his property, especially after incriminating letters were discovered in which Wolsey requested that the Pope excommunicate Henry if Anne was not dismissed from court.

Instead of being reinstated, Wolsey was summoned to trial. However, he escaped the possibility of execution when he died at Leicester in November 1530, on his way to the trial.

The role of the Reformation Parliament

The parliament summoned in October 1529 was bitterly anti-clerical and Wolsey was regarded as the greatest example of an immoral cleric. Henry was also inclined to let the Parliament criticise Wolsey since it justified the actions he took against him.

The charge of praemunire that was imposed on Wolsey was extended to the whole clergy. Henry used the charge to threaten the entire Church. This put pressure on the Pope to give into Henry.

The 1529 Parliament cannot be seen as entirely responsible for Wolsey's downfall, but it did add to the legitimacy of the charges.

Essential notes

Cardinal Campeggio was an Italian cardinal and politician. He had been appointed by Wolsey to the Bishopric of Salisbury so Wolsey believed he could rely on him. However, Campeggio was instructed by the Pope not to reach a decision in the annulment case. Pope Clement did not necessarily want to deny Henry his annulment, but he could not afford to offend Charles V, who still had troops in Rome and was the head of Catherine's family.

Essential notes

Praemunire was a treasonable offence in which the perpetrator is accused of answering first to a foreign power – in this case the Pope.

Examiners' notes

These pages provide you with the opportunity to consider the range of factors that led to Wolsey's fall. You will need to know them in depth. You will then need to move beyond the description to weigh up the relative significance of each cause. Note, for example, that Peter Gwyn dismisses the significance of the factions as the driving force.

The King's 'Great Matter': Why Henry sought an annulment

In the latter years of the 1520s, Henry became convinced that his marriage to Catherine of Aragon was invalid. The consequences of this were far reaching for the English Church and state: in the 1530s, Henry broke with Rome and replaced the authority of the Pope with the Royal Supremacy. This action pushed the English Church on the path to reformation.

The succession problem

- By the mid-1520s, Henry's marriage had failed to produce the much desired son. Princess Mary, born in 1516, was the only surviving child from Catherine's frequent pregnancies.

- There was no precedent in England for female succession; the only attempt had been by Matilda in the 12th century and that had plunged England into twenty years of civil war.

- Henry's own father had taken the crown by force in the civil war commonly known as the War of the Roses. The security of the succession was a priority for Henry to secure his kingdom against a repeat of those events.

Catherine's age

Catherine's last pregnancy was in 1518. By the mid-1520s she was menopausal. It was evident that, as she approached 40 years of age, she would not bear Henry a son. Henry clearly recognised this and stopped sleeping with her in 1524.

Mary's legitimacy

The security of the throne was already threatened by Mary's sex. This problem was compounded by doubts that arose about her legitimacy:

- When Charles V renounced his betrothal to Mary by marrying Isabella of Portugal in 1526, rumours circulated that he had doubts about Mary's legitimacy.

- The same issue arose when a marriage was proposed between Mary and Francis I. The French made enquiries into the validity of the papal dispensation that had been granted to allow Henry and Catherine to marry.

These actions no doubt confirmed the suspicions that were growing in Henry's own mind that he was not legally married to Catherine and that his daughter was a bastard.

Henry's religious doubts

Henry now claimed to have grave doubts that the papal dispensation that had enabled him to marry Catherine was valid, since it contradicted the Bible.

By 1525, Henry's study of passages from Leviticus convinced him that Catherine was not his wife. Leviticus proclaimed that it was unlawful for a man to marry his brother's wife, and that the punishment for this was childlessness. This, Henry declared, explained why his sons by Catherine had died.

Essential notes

'Great Matter' is the term given to Henry's pursuit of the annulment. It was the most significant policy pursued between 1527 and 1533, and it occupied much government attention.

Essential notes

Catherine's first husband was Henry's brother Prince Arthur, who had died in 1502. Before Henry married Catherine in 1509, he had to obtain a papal dispensation because the couple were related as a consequence of Catherine's first marriage. Pope Julius II granted the dispensation on the basis that her marriage to Arthur had been consummated.

Henry used the Hebrew translation of the Bible to strengthen the argument – this version claimed a man would have no sons and so overcame the difficulty that Mary had survived.

The role and significance of Anne Boleyn

The importance of Anne Boleyn in Henry's desire for an annulment is a factor that is hotly debated:

- The historical evidence suggests that Wolsey had no appreciation of Henry's infatuation for Anne when he began proceedings to achieve the annulment.

- Eric Ives, Anne's biographer, suggests that it was not until 1527 that Wolsey realised the extent of Henry's attachment to Anne.

- It is thus more than likely that Anne was not the original motivation, but as time progressed she became increasingly important.

Anne was the second daughter of Thomas Boleyn, Henry's ambassador to France, and the niece of the Duke of Norfolk. She was largely educated in the French court and returned to England as a lady in waiting to Catherine in 1522.

At some time over the new few years, Anne caught Henry's eye. She was no great beauty, but she did have a remarkable personality; in particular, she was unlike the other women at court in that she refused Henry's attentions and insisted that she would not become his mistress.

Anne promised sons to the man she would marry, but Henry would have to be free from his marriage before he could sleep with her. By 1527, it appears that Henry was convinced that his marriage must be annulled so he could marry Anne.

Henry's need for an annulment could be summarised in the following way:

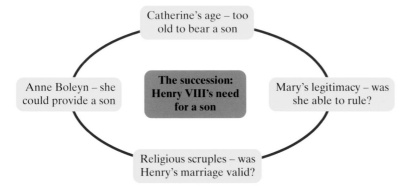

A summary of Henry's need for an annulment of his marriage to Catherine of Aragon

Essential notes

Henry's interpretation of the Bible was confirmed in his mind by the fact that he had an illegitimate son by his mistress, Bessie Blount. This proved there was no impediment to him fathering a son; rather, his failure to do so with Catherine was because God was punishing him for his sins.

Essential notes

Initially, Henry set Wolsey to work, confident that he would achieve the desired result. Later, when the case ran into difficulties, he pursued the annulment through official channels and used informal pressure, such as threats to Churchmen and property, to persuade the Pope to grant his demand.

Examiners' notes

Drawing diagrams such as this is an excellent technique for developing revision notes. Start with the central problem – in this case, the succession. Around this write down the other key factors that played a role in motivating Henry to seek an annulment. Note how these played different roles in the development of the case; for example, it is suggested that Henry's religious scruples were initially more important in initiating proceedings than his infatuation with Anne Boleyn.

The annulment strategy

By 1527, Henry was clear that an annulment was the only solution to his problem. He expected that it could be achieved within a matter of months. Anne was equally confident; by August, she believed that she was a queen in waiting.

> **Source 1**
> (From Angela Anderson & Tony Imperato, *An Introduction to Tudor England 1485–1603*, published by Hodder & Stoughton 2001)
>
> Both men [Henry and Wolsey] assumed it would be a relatively easy task to persuade the Pope to allow Wolsey to hear the divorce case in England, so that the preferred verdict could be delivered.

Wolsey's secret court, May 1527

Wolsey was instructed in May 1527 to begin legal proceedings to free Henry from his invalid marriage:

- He set up a secret tribunal at Westminster. Catherine was not informed about these proceedings and seems to have been generally ignorant of the king's intentions.
- Archbishop Warham was called to confirm that Henry had been living in sin with Catherine for eighteen years.
- The validity of the papal dispensation was attacked.

It is possible that Wolsey may well have been planning to present both Catherine and Rome with a *fait accompli* that the marriage had been found invalid. However, when the news arrived that Rome had been sacked and that the Pope was in captivity, Wolsey abandoned the tribunal.

Catherine's opposition

Catherine was shocked by Henry's declaration to her that they had been living in fornication for eighteen years and that his conscience could no longer allow the situation to continue. She burst into tears and vehemently denied that there was any impediment to her marriage. She maintained that she had been pure when she married Henry.

Catherine never deviated from this claim over the many years it took for Henry to achieve his annulment. Henry was not inclined to care about the opinion of others, but Catherine's family connections did complicate the matter significantly.

Catherine's next step was to inform her nephew, the Emperor Charles V. His control over the Pope and the situation in Rome would ensure that the annulment would drag on for years and not be settled within a few months, as Henry had originally expected.

Wolsey's strategy: the assumption of papal powers

Wolsey's decision to suspend the tribunal in the summer of 1527 may be because he had decided on a new strategy that he believed would bring a quick success and which could not be disputed. Since the Pope was incapacitated in Rome, Wolsey suggested that he assumed his powers as an 'acting pope'.

In order to achieve the position of 'acting pope', Wolsey needed the support of the French cardinals in Avignon. In July 1527 he therefore set off to France with this scheme in mind.

Wolsey also appears to have been ignorant of Henry's desire to marry Anne, because he took with him the proposal that Henry would marry a French princess once the annulment had been pronounced.

Wolsey's comments in the source below make it quite clear that he realised the 'Great Matter' had become a strand of international diplomacy.

Source 2
(From a letter sent by Wolsey to Henry VIII from France in July 1527)

Musing on your Grace's great affair, I consider that the Pope's consent must be gained, in case the Queen rejects my authority. For that, he must be freed, which cannot be achieved except by a peace between the Emperor and the French King. That is unlikely because the Emperor's terms are so harsh. If the Pope were free, I have no doubt that he would easily be persuaded to do what you want.

Wolsey's diplomatic revolution of 1525–26 had put England in the wrong camp, and this is realised in Wolsey's comments above. The capture of the French king (see page 27) weakened England's position. In the end, Wolsey's scheme failed – the French cardinals would not agree to Wolsey's proposition and the strategy had reached a deadlock.

Wolsey's case for the annulment

The case of the annulment was now essentially in the hands of the Pope.

Wolsey was very aware that there were flaws in the king's argument, and he attempted to repair this by persuading Henry of an alternative. Wolsey wanted to steer away from the Bible and focus instead on the validity of Julius II's dispensation.

- If Catherine's claim that she was a virgin when she married Henry was accepted as true, then the dispensation was flawed since it assumed that the marriage had been consummated.

- This argument had the merit that it accepted both the argument of Henry and Catherine, and therefore put the blame for the dispute on the shoulders of the papacy.

- Its great weakness, however, was that the error could be repaired quite easily by the issue of a new dispensation that would validate the current marriage.

- This, of course, was not what Henry wanted. Therefore Wolsey was instructed to pursue the case based on Henry's arguments and not his own.

Examiners' notes

In analysing a source of this nature, it is important to consider Wolsey's purpose in writing it. It is possible to infer from the text that Wolsey is seeking to excuse the failure of the annulment case by focusing on diplomatic problems. Wolsey's involvement in managing Henry's diplomacy perhaps explains why he ends this extract with such an optimistic note; that the Pope would be willing to grant the annulment. This would help deflect criticism from him.

Examiners' notes

The events of the Great Matter are intrinsically linked with foreign policy. This is why it is essential that you do not revise topics in isolation but establish the links between them.

Essential notes

The term 'related in the first degree of affinity' used by Peter Gwyn refers to Henry's relationship with Anne's sister Mary. At the time, canon (Church) law stated that there was an affinity or relationship between a man and the blood relatives of the woman with whom he was sleeping. Mary Boleyn was Henry's mistress sometime between 1521 and 1526. She bore two children, but Henry did not acknowledge them and we cannot be certain that they were his. Nevertheless, Mary's relationship with Henry meant that he was related to Anne.

Examiners' notes

Gwyn highlights a key flaw in Henry's argument for an annulment – that he was related to Catherine by marriage and so had broken God's law. His previous relationship with Anne's sister casts a doubt as to whether his religious scruples were really his motivation for seeking an annulment. This is a useful opinion to consider when you are weighing up the relative significance both of the reasons why he sought an annulment and also why he failed to get papal approval.

Why the annulment strategy failed

Henry's confidence that his annulment could be achieved in a matter of months soon proved to be unfounded. The case dragged on for years and would only be settled by Henry's break from the Catholic Church.

The weaknesses of Henry's strategy

Henry based his strategy on his interpretation of the Bible. He claimed that Leviticus stated that his marriage to Catherine was invalid because she was his brother's widow. However, there were significant problems with this approach:

- The passage in Leviticus refers to a living wife not a widow, and he and Catherine did have a living child – Mary.
- Henry's argument was also undermined by Deuteronomy, which states that a man can marry his brother's widow and raise sons for him.

By rejecting Deuteronomy in favour of his own interpretation of the Bible, Henry weakened his position. Furthermore, his arguments looked flimsy as it became more obvious that Henry was driven by his lust for Anne. It seemed increasingly as though Henry wanted to cast off the old wife to bring in the new.

> **Source 3**
> (From Peter Gwyn, *The King's Cardinal: The Rise and Fall of Thomas Wolsey*, published by Pimlico 1992)
>
> Henry's request to be free to marry someone to whom he was related in the first degree of affinity could only confirm the rumour that his 'scruple' had little to do with God and more to do with Anne Boleyn, who as a consequence of Henry's affair with her sister Mary, was related to the king in just that degree. By drawing attention to Anne, it made it difficult for the Pope to take seriously any more acceptable reasons that might be advanced later for dispensing with the first marriage.

Henry's relationship with Mary Boleyn completely undermined his reliance on biblical arguments. The strategy he pursued was flawed because Scripture offered an alternative and arguably more convincing alternative and, combined with the restrictions placed on the Pope as a result of the Sack of Rome, it was unlikely to succeed.

The consequences of the Sack of Rome

Pope Clement was kept prisoner in Castel Sant' Angelo for six months until he escaped in October 1527. However, the presence of imperial troops in Rome meant that he could not act freely, and most importantly, he could not afford to offend Charles V.

Roger Lockyer and Dan Sullivan (Source 4) believe this was the most significant reason why Henry did not get his annulment.

Source 4
(From R. Lockyer and D. O'Sullivan, *Tudor Britain*, published by Longman 1997)

Normally the Pope would have been happy to please someone as important as Henry. Annulments were not uncommon among the rich and powerful. But in this case there was one snag. In May 1527 an Imperial army had sacked Rome, and after this the Pope was under the control of Charles V, who was Catherine of Aragon's nephew. Pope Clement did not want to offend Henry, but still less could he afford to offend Charles by allowing Henry to humiliate Charles's aunt.

The Sack of Rome thus added a significant complication to a case that was already weak. Clement stalled in Rome, hoping that if he did not reach a solution then either Henry would tire of Anne or Catherine would die. Eventually, he proposed two solutions:

- He would legitimise any illegitimate children born to Henry and Anne.
- He would sanction a marriage between Princess Mary and Henry Fitzroy, Henry's illegitimate son by Bessie Blount.

For his part, Henry hoped to persuade the Pope of the justice of his case, and suggested that he supply 2000 troops to protect him. However, Clement rejected this obviously intimidatory tactic.

The court at Blackfriars: Catherine's opposition and the role of Campeggio

The annulment was to be decided at Blackfriars Court in London, in May 1529. Henry was optimistic that the court would rule in his favour; the presiding judges were to be Cardinal Wolsey and Cardinal Campeggio, whom Henry believed was sympathetic to his plight.

The case turned out to be a disaster for Henry:

- Catherine rejected Campeggio's previous proposal that she retire to a nunnery. She insisted that she would live and die in a state of matrimony.
- Catherine unexpectedly produced a copy of her dispensation obtained from Spain, of which the English had been quite unaware. It differed slightly from the English version and so added an additional legal complication.
- Catherine refused to acknowledge the validity of the court. After appealing her case to Rome, she refused to attend court again.
- Henry's case was reduced to farce, as the only evidence was hearsay from witnesses who claimed Arthur had boasted of sleeping with Catherine the morning after his marriage.

Campeggio took advantage of Catherine's appeal and suspended the court for the summer recess observed in Rome. Henry had made no progress in achieving his annulment, and on October 9 1529 Wolsey was dismissed.

Examiners' notes

This source suggests it was the power of Charles V combined with the failure of Henry's foreign policy that doomed Henry's attempt to win a papal annulment. Henry's rejection of the Hapsburg alliance in 1525–6 meant that Catherine and not he gained the support of Charles V. The source highlights the links between the Great Matter and foreign policy. If we compare the opinion expressed here with that in Source 3, we can see that the authors regard the international situation as far more significant than the weakness of Henry's strategy.

Essential notes

Lorenzo Campeggio had been previously rewarded for service with the Bishopric of Salisbury, so it is not surprising that Henry thought he was on his side. He was unaware that Campeggio had been instructed by Clement to stall for time and not reach a decision.

Examiners' notes

This is a topic where you will need to weigh up the relative significance of the causes. This requires careful reasoning. Would Henry have achieved his annulment if his case had been stronger, or was the power of Charles V and his relationship to Catherine always going to prevent this?

The role of the Reformation Parliament, 1529–32

The failure of the court at Blackfriars to settle the Great Matter pushed policy into a state of disarray. In October 1529, Henry summoned a parliament without really knowing in which direction to proceed. The period between 1529 and 1532 has sometimes been called 'the years without a policy' because there was no immediate solution to the deadlock.

Definition of the Reformation Parliament

- The Parliament that Henry summoned in 1529 is known as the Reformation Parliament, although that title was not actually used until the 19th century.

- The Reformation Parliament sat for seven years. This was longer than any parliament sat before 1529. Its lengthy sitting allowed it to develop many procedures that we now associate with parliament.

- In time, this Parliament would pass legislation that was vital to the English Reformation, but this role was not apparent in the early sittings.

Anti-clericalism: Attack on Wolsey and the Church

At the opening of the Reformation Parliament, it was obvious that Henry had no clear plan.

The Parliament began with an attack on Wolsey that justified Henry's dismissal of his former favourite and led to the charge of praemunire (the accusation that Wolsey had committed treason by answering to the Pope before the king).

Source 5
(From Articles of Impeachment exhibited in Parliament against Cardinal Wolsey, 6 November 1529)

Constrained by the necessity of our fidelity and conscience, [we] complain and show to your majesty that the lord cardinal of York, lately your grace's chancellor, presuming to take upon him the authority of the pope's legate 'de latare' hath by diverse and many sundry ways and fashions, committed notable high and grievous offences, misusing, altering and subverting the order of your grace's laws.

These complaints then proceeded into a general criticism of the Church. Some MPs in the Commons had sympathy with the anti-clerical arguments being put forward by writers such as William Tyndale and Simon Fish, who were highly critical of the state of the Church and clergy in England:

- Henry did not intend at this stage to implement a reformation in the Church, but the prevailing sentiments were useful in getting rid of Wolsey who had failed him.

- In addition, Henry may have had a vague idea that the Parliament could declare his marriage to Catherine invalid, but no progress was made in this direction in the first sitting.

Essential notes

The Reformation Parliament did not sit for seven years without a break. The king frequently suspended or prorogued (discontinued) its sittings when it was not needed. Indeed, it was suspended for longer than it sat, which was only 484 days in six and a half years. Henry did not dismiss the Parliament, since this would necessitate fresh elections before parliament could sit again.

Examiners' notes

Read this contemporary source carefully.
16th-century language can be difficult to understand, but you should usually be able to recognise the general sentiment. For example, words such as 'complain', 'grievous offences' and 'subverting' all indicate that the source is critical of Wolsey. You also need to use your understanding of the context in which the source was produced to help you interpret it. By applying criticisms of Wolsey's clerical offences, such as pluralism and absenteeism and the accusations that he considered himself to be the equal of kings, you will be able to develop your analysis.

Why was little progress made in Parliament in 1529?

Henry's decision to call parliament should have precipitated some action to address the Great Matter, but instead policy seemed to be in a state of limbo. The reasons for this are displayed on the diagram below.

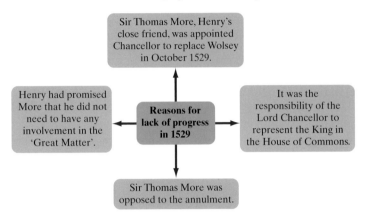

Sir Thomas More, Henry's close friend, was appointed Chancellor to replace Wolsey in October 1529.

Henry had promised More that he did not need to have any involvement in the 'Great Matter'.

Reasons for lack of progress in 1529

It was the responsibility of the Lord Chancellor to represent the King in the House of Commons.

Sir Thomas More was opposed to the annulment.

Reasons for the lack of progress in 1529. Note that Thomas More was a key reason.

The role of Thomas Cromwell

The key figure who would eventually find a way out of the quagmire was Thomas Cromwell.

- He was first elected MP in 1523 and gained prominence in Wolsey's service.

- In 1529, he realised that loyalty to the king would have to surpass any loyalties to his former master, Thomas Wolsey. Cromwell defended Wolsey in Parliament, but cautioned Wolsey to accept his lot and did not succeed in fulfilling Wolsey's pleas that he should restore him to the king's favour.

- Cromwell was elected to the 1529 Parliament as the member for Taunton. He was not immediately influential in the proceedings of that Parliament, but sometime during this period he rose in the king's favour.

- In 1530, Cromwell was appointed to the Royal Council.

By the time the third session of the Reformation Parliament began its sitting in January 1531, the idea of a Royal Supremacy over the Church, which would enable Henry to grant his own annulment, was gaining credence. Cromwell was one of the foremost supporters of this strategy.

The 1532 Parliament thus began with a thorough assault on the freedoms and privileges of the Church. Thomas Cromwell was the man who steered the policy through Parliament. In particular, he used his position in parliament to force the clergy to submit to the authority of the king.

Examiners' notes

Study the spider diagram. Visual representations can be a useful way of revising and recalling information. Note that there are four key points relating to Sir Thomas More's role in undermining the chances of finding a solution.

Essential notes

The Submission of the Clergy is dealt with in detail on pages 46–47. The clergy was forced to agree that the king was Head of the Church in England and to pay a substantial fine.

The Submission of the Clergy, 1531–32

Henry's attempt to achieve his annulment by papal authority had reached a dead end by the early 1530s. Yet he was determined to have his own way.

As early as 1515, Henry had questioned whether the clergy were truly his subjects if they also owed allegiance to Rome. By 1531, he had come to believe that the clergy must answer to him alone. Henry also believed that forcing them to submit to his authority would provide the pressure he needed to force the Pope's hand.

Henry's developing ideas on the authority of the Church

The idea that the king was the supreme authority in his own realm was not a new idea, but it had gained increasing influence in the European Reformation. By 1531, Henry found it very persuasive. The key ideas are summarised below.

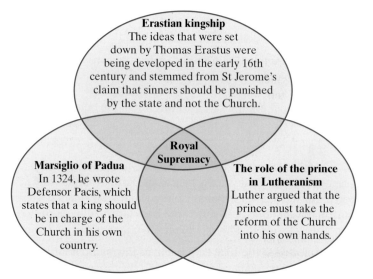

Ideas of royal supremacy

Erastian kingship
The ideas that were set down by Thomas Erastus were being developed in the early 16th century and stemmed from St Jerome's claim that sinners should be punished by the state and not the Church.

Marsiglio of Padua
In 1324, he wrote Defensor Pacis, which states that a king should be in charge of the Church in his own country.

Royal Supremacy

The role of the prince in Lutheranism
Luther argued that the prince must take the reform of the Church into his own hands.

Cranmer's solutions

While Henry was developing his ideas on the extent of his authority over the Church, new solutions were put forward to the king by a rising cleric in the Boleyn faction – Thomas Cranmer.

- Cranmer suggested that the case was not a legal one; rather, it was theologians and not the Pope who could supply the judgement. He was commissioned to visit the great universities of Europe and canvass their opinions. Seven universities gave a favourable opinion, after they had received bribes.

- Cranmer compiled a collection of old English manuscripts (known as *Collectanea satis copiosa*) dating back to the Anglo Saxon period, which supported Henry's ideas on the supreme authority of the monarch over the Church.

Cranmer's contributions did not provide a final solution to the problem, but they did help Henry on the route to success by demonstrating that he was not seeking new powers but merely claiming authority that was historically his own to exercise.

Pressure on the Church: The fining of the clergy, 1531

Henry believed that applying the correct pressure on the Church would force the clergy to submit to his authority, and that this would enable him to get his annulment. Therefore, in January 1531, the whole clergy was charged with the treasonable offence of praemunire.

It was impossible for the clergy to deny the charge, since each cleric had taken an oath to the papacy. When the Convocation of the Church met, it was told that it could avoid the charge if it agreed to grant the following to the King:

* £100 000

* the title Supreme Head of the Church in England and Wales.

The Convocation had little choice but to agree in return for Henry's pardon. They promised to pay the fine over five years, but added to the title 'as far as the word of Christ allows'. This did leave the title open to interpretation, which reduced its effect, although it was not long before this addition was forgotten.

The supplication against the ordinaries, 1532

The attack on the clergy inspired the anti-clerical members of the Commons to go further. In early 1532, the House of Commons petitioned the king to take action against clerics who abused their legal powers. This was done in a document known as a 'supplication against the ordinaries'. (The term 'ordinary' refers to a bishop and other clergy with the authority to exercise jurisdiction.)

Whether this was spontaneous or engineered by Cromwell is unclear, but it gave Henry a welcome opportunity to attack the legal independence of the Church. Henry demanded that:

* all future change in canon law would require the consent of the monarch

* canon law that contradicted the royal prerogative must be annulled.

These demands swept away the independence of the Church and the authority of the papacy.

The Submission of the Clergy, May 1532

The attack on the Church rendered it virtually powerless. Although Archbishop Warham tried to rally himself against the onslaught, and men like Bishop John Fisher of Rochester would never submit, the clergy's resistance had been broken. They feared a charge of treason.

Therefore, in May 1532, the Convocation voted through the Submission of the Clergy. Many members absented themselves from the vote, but this made little difference to Henry. The Submission of the Clergy meant that the English Church was placed under royal control.

Henry had not yet achieved his annulment, but he now knew that the clergy would not oppose it. His Chancellor, Sir Thomas More, resigned.

Essential notes

The Convocations of the Church were meetings of the bishops of the two provinces, Canterbury and York. They were always summoned when a parliament was summoned. The Convocation was at this time presided over by Warham, the Archbishop of Canterbury.

Essential notes

The origins of this caveat or addition to the title have been debated by historians. It used to be thought that this was an example of Archbishop Warham rallying to the cause of the Church, but some historians now claim that Henry's advisers added it, knowing that it would placate the conservative clergy and that it would, in any case, be ignored.

Examiners' notes

It is important that you can explain the significance of the supplication against the ordinaries. It marked a key stage in progress towards establishing a Royal Supremacy that would enable Henry to sanction his annulment himself.

Royal Supremacy and the Break with Rome, 1532–34

The Royal Supremacy refers to Henry's control of the Church. It would remove the authority of the Pope in England and establish the absolute control of the monarch over religion, both the organisational structure and the doctrine and practices of the Church.

The role and importance of parliament

One of the most important features of the Royal Supremacy was that it was established by the passing of statute law in parliament, which was the highest form of law. The fact that the Royal Supremacy was established in parliament gave the king's powers great weight because they had the agreement of the political nation behind them. It was not a case of the king unilaterally assuming powers that might be disputed.

The role of parliament was essential. Although the clergy had submitted and agreed that the king was 'Supreme Head of the Church in England and Wales', the caveat 'as far as the word of Christ allows' left an ambiguity in the claim that needed to be settled.

Act in Conditional Restraint of Annates, 1532

This Act was the first stage in establishing the Royal Supremacy and was to cut England's ties to Rome. There were two key terms:

- an end to the payment of annates to the Papacy (these payments were made by bishops when they were first appointed)
- bishops could be consecrated by English authority.

It is possible that, at this stage, Henry still hoped that financial pressure would force the Pope to give him his annulment.

However, the Act did not change the attitude of the Pope. By the end of 1532, evidence suggests that Henry doubted that his Great Matter would be settled by Rome. The way forward was now through legislation passed by a willing parliament.

Act in Restraint of Appeals, 1533

The Act in Restraint of Appeals was passed in March 1533. By this time, Anne Boleyn had finally given in to Henry's demands and fallen pregnant sometime in December 1532. They were married by Cranmer, the newly appointed Archbishop of Canterbury. Cranmer could justify marrying the couple before annulling Henry's marriage to Catherine, since the argument was always that the marriage was invalid and therefore Henry was a free man.

The Act set out Henry's legal position as head of the English Church:

- All legal cases, even of a spiritual nature, could be settled in England.
- There was no right of appeal to Rome.
- The King was the supreme authority in all legal cases.

One of the reasons why the Act was accepted was that it claimed that these powers had always belonged to the King of England, so they were not new.

Source 6
(Adapted from the Act in Restraint of Appeals, 1533)

This realm of England is an empire, and so has been accepted in the world, governed by one supreme head and king having the dignity and royal estate of the imperial crown of the same. He is furnished by the goodness and sufferance of Almighty God with plenary, whole and entire power to render justice and make final determination in all causes occurring within this realm without the interference of any foreign prince.

The Act's most important purpose in the first instance was to prevent Catherine from appealing her case to Rome. Cranmer thus pronounced that Henry's first marriage was null and void.

The more far-reaching significance is that, in the long run, it:

- established Henry's supreme authority over the Church
- absolutely severed ties between the Church in England and Wales and the Roman Catholic Church.

Act of Succession, 1534
Instead of the long awaited son, Anne's pregnancy resulted in a daughter, Elizabeth, who was born in September 1533. However, Henry was optimistic that a son would come next.

It was essential that the rights of succession to the throne were settled. The Act of Succession, passed in 1534, declared:

- Henry's only heirs were his children by Anne Boleyn.
- Princess Mary was illegitimate.
- All subjects must take an oath to ensure that they agreed with the Act.
- Those who denied the succession would be punished by death.

Act of Supremacy, 1534
The Act of Supremacy reaffirmed the message in the Act in Restraint of Appeals – Henry was Supreme Head of the Church in England and Wales, and the Bishop of Rome (as the Pope was now called) had no authority.

Treasons Act, 1534
It was treasonable to deny the Acts of Supremacy and Succession. Cromwell ensured that there could be no doubt as to the nature of treason by introducing this new Act into parliament.

Before 1534, the charge of treason was levied against those who intended to deprive the king of his powers or life by their actions, including what they had written. The new Act stated that it was treasonable to oppose the Royal Supremacy by the spoken word.

It was an important mechanism in keeping the people loyal, and it marked another extension of royal authority. It was also an essential piece of legislation, because in September 1534 the Pope threatened to excommunicate Henry.

Examiners' notes

Examine the text of this Act carefully. David Loades claims that the Act in Restraint of Appeals is an example of Cromwell moving slowly towards the Supremacy. The Act established the king's legal control of the Church and ensured the legitimacy of Henry's children with Anne. It is a key stage in the establishment of the Royal Supremacy.

Essential notes

The Royal Supremacy strengthened the powers of the king in these ways:

- all subjects, including the clergy, were brought under the king's authority
- the authority of the Pope in England was completely removed
- Henry's financial position was improved by claiming the annates previously paid to the Pope
- Henry was able to impose his will by: marrying Anne; annulling his marriage; legitimising his heirs by Anne
- Henry was able to enforce his Supremacy by punishing deniers of the Supremacy and the Succession under the Treasons Act.

The roles of Cromwell, Cranmer and Anne Boleyn in establishing the Royal Supremacy

The concept of the prince directing religious policy in his realm was not a new idea. It was in fact a key reformist issue in the early 16th century.

Henry did not arrive at this solution alone. In 1521, he had fully supported the papal supremacy in his *Assertio Septum*. It was the urgency of his case, coupled with the intransigence of the Pope, that made Henry receptive to the advice and suggestions of key figures around him. The most influential were Anne Boleyn and members of her faction, Thomas Cromwell and Thomas Cranmer.

The influence of Anne Boleyn

Anne clearly had an ulterior motive for pushing Henry towards the Royal Supremacy. Indeed, after the failure of the Blackfriars Court, it seemed the only option if she were to succeed in marrying the king.

Anne had been brought up in the French Court, where she had adopted reformist ideas. She was not a Lutheran (as some historians claim), but she was definitely evangelical. She shared her views and the sources she read with Henry:

- William Tyndale's *Obedience of the Christian Man* claimed that in early Christian history it was kings who controlled the Church, not foreign authorities like the Pope. Tyndale was a known heretic, but according to the historian David Loades, Anne did not reveal this to Henry.

- Simon Fish's *Supplication of Beggars* was an anti-clerical tract that emphasised the way in which the clergy evaded the king's justice by maintaining their own court system. Henry pardoned Fish for his heresy.

- Christopher St Germain was an English lawyer. In his *Treatise Concerning the Division between the Spirituality and Temporality*, he argued that Henry had the right to govern the Church in his kingdom.

The king read these sources and it is likely that they played a role in persuading him that unless he took control of the Church, his powers would always be compromised.

Anne was therefore an important figure in pushing Henry on the path towards the Supremacy, not only because she was determined to marry him, but also because she introduced him to ideas that encouraged him to take complete control of the Church.

The role of Thomas Cranmer

- It was Cranmer who had broken the deadlock in the king's case in autumn 1529 by suggesting that it could be solved by theologians and not canon lawyers.

- He also gathered the views from Europe's leading universities in the winter and spring of 1529–30.

- In addition, he compiled documents from old English sources in the *Collectanae satis copiosa*.

Although this did not immediately result in the desired annulment, Henry made Cranmer the new Archbishop of Canterbury in 1533. As Archbishop of Canterbury, Cranmer held a seat in the House of Lords and was able to promote the legislation that established the Royal Supremacy. It was Cranmer who pronounced Henry's first marriage null and void.

Cranmer was at this time a relatively junior member of Henry's court, but his importance in finding the arguments that justified Henry's assertion of control over the Church should not be underestimated.

Cromwell and the Royal Supremacy

Thomas Cromwell is the key figure in creating the Royal Supremacy. Cromwell was a lawyer and evangelical reformer. Anne provided Henry with access to ideas and Cranmer provided the argument, but it was Cromwell who helped draft the legislation and drive the bills through parliament to become statute law.

Source 7
(From Alan G. R. Smith, *The Emergence of a Nation State 1529–1660*, published by Longman 1997)

Cromwell gave a new drive and determination to the royal plans and played the dominant role in drawing up the detailed anti-papal legislation of 1532–4 and putting it through Parliament. The minds of both king and minister were therefore of the greatest importance in the accomplishment of the schism [split from Rome].

In seven sessions of the Reformation Parliament, Cromwell steered through a great volume of legislation that broke the English ties to Rome, established the Royal Supremacy and moved England on the path to Protestant reform. The most significant Act was the Act in Restraint of Appeals, which David Loades claims had Cromwell's fingerprints all over it.

Cromwell was therefore essential in the process of establishing the Royal Supremacy.

Anne Boleyn	Thomas Cranmer	Thomas Cromwell

Supplied ideas from writers who criticised the clergy and emphasised the authority of the prince in his own realm	Provided the arguments and documents that justified the king's position	Used parliament to push through the legislation that freed the king from Rome and established the Royal Supremacy

The contributions of Anne Boleyn, Cranmer and Cromwell

The development of Protestant ideas

The period after 1533 witnessed the introduction of reformist ideas and practices in England that had characterised the Protestant Reformation in Europe. The pace of change varied across the period and the Henrician Church that emerged was in many ways unique – a combination of Catholic and Protestant ideas that reflected the desires of the king as well as the influence of key members of his court.

In order to understand the impact of the Reformation, it is necessary to first identify the key differences between Catholicism and Protestantism and then to consider what changes were introduced into England.

Church hierarchy

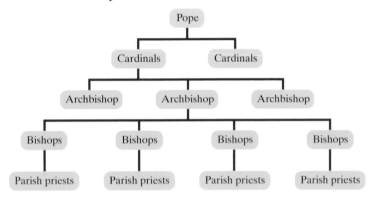

Essential notes

This shows a very simplified version of the hierarchy of the Catholic Church. Although the Pope would take recommendations from the head of state, the consecration of archbishops and bishops was a papal right.

Catholic Church hierarchy

Essential notes

The clergy consisted of several types. Rectors claimed both greater and lesser tithes in the parish and supervised parish priests. Vicar was the title given to certain parish priests who exercised authority under the rector's supervision. The position of vicar was established by law and supported by lesser tithes (10% of the wealth of parishioners). Curates were supported by a small salary.

The simplified hierarchy of the Church in England after the break from Rome shows the most significant difference – as Supreme Head the king was responsible for all appointments. The most important churchman was the Archbishop of Canterbury and he supervised the work of the bishops, who in turn monitored the parish priests, rectors, vicars and curates in their dioceses.

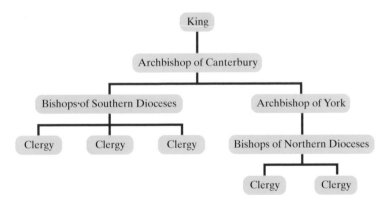

Church of England hierarchy

The role of the clergy

The table below outlines key differences in the role of the clergy.

Catholic	Protestant
Consecrated and therefore regarded as superior to parishioners	Regarded as an equal member of the community
Necessary to intercede between the individual and God and to interpret the Bible for parishioners	Responsible for preaching the word of God
Celibate	Clerical marriage permitted

Church layout and decoration

The changes in the English Church came gradually. It is likely that by the end of Henry's reign, in most churches the layout did not differ from that which had existed for centuries under the Catholic Church.

The table below indicates some of the potential changes in Church layout and decoration.

Catholic	Protestant
Highly decorated vestments worn by the priest	Plain surplice worn by the vicar
Decorated interiors with stained glass windows and wall paintings	Plain church interiors with only scripture painted on the walls
Highly decorated altar set at the eastern end of the church and railed off from the congregation	Plain communion table that could be approached by the whole community; in some reformed churches it was set in the centre of the church

Doctrine

There were also key differences in the doctrines or beliefs of the Catholic and Protestant Churches. The table below outlines the most important ones.

Catholic	Protestant
Transubstantiation – the bread and wine were turned into the actual body and blood of Christ	Consubstantiation – the doctrine developed by Martin Luther that the body and blood of Christ co-existed with the bread and wine
Only the priest would take communion in both kinds	Communion in both kinds was available for clergy and for laity
The dead were held in purgatory until they had atoned for their sins	There was no evidence in scripture for the existence of purgatory
Confession to a priest was necessary to obtain forgiveness for sins	Private confession to God (there was no need for the intervention of a priest)
Latin Bible	Bible in the vernacular
Salvation could be achieved by faith and good works	Salvation could be achieved by faith alone (*sola fidism*)

Essential notes

The presence of wall paintings and stained glass windows were a vital part of the Catholic Church. Since services were conducted in Latin and very few members of the congregation could read, the people learned their Bible stories through pictures. In the Protestant Church, the emphasis was on studying scripture in your own language (the vernacular). Wall paintings were therefore considered a distraction from the word of God.

Essential notes

Communion in both kinds refers to the bread and wine. In the 16th-century Catholic Church, the congregation received only bread; wine was reserved for the clergy alone.

The doctrine of purgatory was a key element in Catholic teaching. It was believed that souls of the dead went there to be purged of any sins before they could enter heaven.

The factors that influenced religious change

The years 1533–39 were ones of rapid religious change. The Reformation that had spread across Europe for the previous two decades now began to have a significant and lasting impact in England.

While Henry had vigorously opposed attacks on the Church, criticising Luther's beliefs in his *Assertio Septum* in 1521, his marital problems and the stubborn refusal of the papacy to compromise had led him to break with Rome and establish the Royal Supremacy.

Other factors now combined to bring about far reaching changes in the English Church. These are summarised in the diagram below.

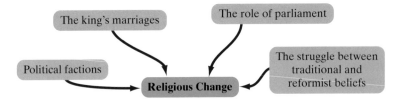

Factors influencing religious change in the English Church under Henry VIII

Political factions

The pro- and anti-Aragonese factions of the 1520s underwent a change. The pro-Aragonese faction continued to support Mary's claims after Catherine's death in 1536. The members of both factions also aligned in new factions. They used religion as a key tool in their struggle to influence royal policy and gain royal favour. (The impact of factions on church reform can be seen on page 60.)

Examiners' notes

Study this diagram closely. Diagrams such as these are useful for summarising key themes, and are very helpful in examinations for planning the key points that you will develop in depth in your answer.

Essential notes

The pro-Aragonese faction supported Catherine during Henry's campaign to achieve his annulment. The anti-Aragonese faction, of which the Boleyns were a part, supported Henry.

The Boleyn faction	The Reformist faction	The Conservative faction
Played a vital role in the initial changes.	Emerged out of the Boleyn faction.	Opposed the pace of change set by the reformists.
Aimed to secure the break with Rome and the Royal Supremacy that would secure Anne's marriage to the king.	Aimed to ensure that the collapse of Henry's marriage to Anne did not push reform off course.	Key members were the Duke of Norfolk and the Bishop of Winchester.
Key members (Anne, Cranmer and Cromwell) were evangelicals who favoured changes such as the availability of scriptures in English.	Key members were Thomas Cromwell and Thomas Cranmer, and later Edward Seymour.	Regarded the Royal Supremacy as the finishing point for reform.
	More radical than the king in their religious beliefs, but careful not to go beyond what the king would find acceptable.	Gained the upper hand in 1539 as a result of the king's dissatisfaction with his marriage to Anne of Cleves.
	Regarded the Royal Supremacy as the starting point for reform.	Promoted orthodox Catholic beliefs in the doctrine and practices of the Church.
	In the mid 1530s, it focused on reforming the doctrine and practices of the Church.	

Henry's marriages

As the diagram on page 54 indicates, Henry's marriages played a key role in the development of religious policy. They were inextricably linked with the factions, since the leaders of the factions were constantly engaged in a struggle to place their candidate before the king in the hope that this would give them greater influence:

- Henry's marriage to Anne Boleyn was a key factor in the initial religious changes.
- Henry's marriage to Anne of Cleves was an attempt by Cromwell to promote further reform in the Church by securing a Protestant alliance.
- Catherine Howard was deliberately dangled before Henry by the Conservatives in order to improve their access to the king and reduce the influence of the reforming faction.

The role of parliament

The Reformation Parliament was essential in religious change for a number of reasons:

- Anti-clericalism in the Reformation Parliament played a significant role in the removal of Cardinal Wolsey in 1529, the Submission of the Clergy in 1532, and the dissolution of the monasteries in 1536–39.
- Many key religious changes were established by statute law, which was the highest form of law so gave real legitimacy to the changes.

Anti-clericalism was greatest in the House of Commons, although it was probably exaggerated by Edward Hall, the 16th-century chronicler and MP.

The Lords was always more inclined to traditional beliefs and initially opposed the Submission of the Clergy. However, it later supported the dissolution of the monasteries, especially as many of its members benefitted from the king's ability to grant former monastic lands to supporters, and the Act of Six Articles in 1539.

The struggle between reformist and traditional beliefs

The key factor emerging here is that a struggle developed between reformist and traditional beliefs. This struggle shaped the development of the Church of England. The two factions played a key role in attempting to secure the ascendency of their religious preferences but the lynchpin in the system was the king.

Henry inclined to traditional beliefs; he preferred the ceremony and doctrines he had learned as a child and defended in 1521. Yet he never deviated from the Royal Supremacy once he had embarked on that path.

Henry's policy was often based on political convenience rather than religious beliefs. For example, he supported the dissolution of the monasteries which enriched his treasury, but he did not endorse the Bishops' Book in 1537 that downgraded the importance of Mass. Henry may also have been worried by the opposition to reform shown in the Pilgrimage of Grace of 1536. Therefore his policy was often driven by a consideration of what would be the greatest political benefit combined with what could be achieved peacefully, rather than a full endorsement of either religious stance.

Essential notes

The dates for Henry's marriages are as follows:

- Catherine of Aragon, 1509–33
- Anne Boleyn, 1533–36
- Jane Seymour, 1536–37
- Anne of Cleves, 1540
- Catherine Howard, 1540–42
- Catherine Parr, 1543–47

Essential notes

Edward Hall's chronicle, *The Union of the Two Noble and Illustrate Families of Lancastre and Yorke*, covers the events in parliament during Henry VIII's reign in great detail. Hall was a member of the Reformation Parliament and so an eyewitness to events. However, historians now treat his chronicle with some care, since Hall's anti-clerical beliefs have coloured his account.

Essential notes

Bishop Gardiner helped draft the Act of Six Articles, which brought an end to religious experimentation and placed more emphasis on traditional beliefs.

The dissolution of the monasteries and the Act of Six Articles are dealt with in full on pages 62–67 and 72–73.

Essential notes

The Bishops' Book and the Pilgrimage of Grace are dealt with in full on pages 67–69.

Opposition to religious change

The first signs of opposition to Henry's religious changes were triggered by his decision to end his marriage to Catherine of Aragon. Henry's response to those who refused to accept the end of his marriage and the Royal Supremacy was brutal, and sent a clear message that he would not compromise.

The Holy Maid of Kent

Elizabeth Barton was a serving girl who was sent to a nunnery after she claimed to have visions. In 1527 she prophesised that Henry would die soon if he married Anne Boleyn.

Barton gained some high profile supporters, including Archbishop Warham and John Fisher, Bishop of Rochester. Even the Chancellor, Sir Thomas More, was consulted about her claims. Her fame spread widely after her supporter, a Canterbury monk called Edward Bocking, published her prophesies in *The Nun's Book* in 1533.

Cromwell, who was placed in charge of the case, responded with a ruthlessness that became typical of Henry's regime. The chance of Elizabeth Barton becoming the centre of a dangerous conspiracy was certainly exaggerated, but the Imperial Ambassador, Eustace Chapuys, was known to be sympathetic and this increased the threat that Charles V might intervene.

Consequently, in 1534, charges were drawn up against Elizabeth and Edward Bocking. They were swiftly found guilty of treason and hanged at Tyburn.

Bishop John Fisher

A more deadly foe than Elizabeth Barton was John Fisher, Bishop of Rochester:

- Fisher had opposed Henry's attempts to annul his marriage to Catherine in books and sermons. He became Catherine's most trusted adviser and counsellor and appeared on her behalf in court.

- In 1532, Fisher refused to sign the Submission of the Clergy and he preached openly against the divorce.

- He was arrested and sent to the Tower in April 1534 for refusing the Royal Supremacy, but Fisher remained steadfast.

- Fisher was tried as a common criminal by a jury, found guilty on evidence from Richard Rich that he had denied the Supremacy, and beheaded at Tower Hill on 22 June 1535.

Sir Thomas More

Thomas More had been Henry's close friend, a man whose advice he respected and followed. When he became Chancellor in 1529, Henry promised More that he need not have any role in the Great Matter. However, it was impossible for More to remain on the sidelines as the king's entire policy revolved around this one goal – to achieve the annulment and marry Anne.

- More resigned the Chancellorship in 1532 over the Submission of the Clergy and promised to retire to a quiet life where he would say and do nothing about the king's affairs.

- However, when the Royal Supremacy and the Act of Succession was passed, Henry was insistent that the great men of the realm should submit. More had an international reputation and therefore his submission was regarded as essential by Henry.

- More refused to take the oath. This was sufficient for him to be arrested and sent to the Tower. However, as a lawyer, More knew that he could not be executed unless he actually denied the Supremacy. Therefore he maintained his silence in prison for a year.

- When More was finally convicted, it was on insufficient evidence given by Richard Rich, who claimed that More had denied that parliament had the right to pass a law that declared the king Supreme Head of the Church.

- More was executed on 6 July 1535.

The Observant Friars and Carthusian Monks

Most religious orders accepted the Royal Supremacy, but these two stand out for their opposition. Their refusal to renounce allegiance to Rome led to the most severe punishments.

> **Source 1**
> (From Derek Wilson, *A Brief History of Henry VIII: Reformer and Tyrant*, published by Robinson 2009)
>
> Those who refused the oath were sent to prison where many of them died. The rest were relocated to the houses of their rivals, the Conventional Franciscans where, it is claimed, they were treated worse than if they had been locked up in the Tower.

The three priors of the Carthusian monks were executed at Tyburn by hanging, drawing and quartering, while the remaining members of the order were imprisoned in the Tower. Ten of them starved to death there.

The treatment of the monks is a clear sign that not only would Henry not tolerate opposition, he would punish opponents with the utmost brutality.

> **Source 2**
> (From Derek Wilson, *A Brief History of Henry VIII: Reformer and Tyrant*, published by Robinson 2009)
>
> This orgy of blood-letting needs to be explained. There is no doubt that the responsibility lies squarely with Henry...Cranmer tried hard to persuade him to allow More and Fisher to subscribe to a modified form of the oath but Henry would not budge.

Essential notes

Rich claimed that More denied the Royal Supremacy in conversation with him in his prison cell. There were no other witnesses but More's insistence on maintaining complete silence on the matter since his resignation as Chancellor makes this unlikely. However, Rich is reputed to have tricked More into giving a private opinion that More regarded as something like a confessional and so presumed that Rich would not reveal.

Examiners' notes

Study these two sources from Derek Wilson. They are both focused on the punishments imposed on the opposition. The first, however, is a descriptive source; it is providing information about what happened. The second extract offers opinion; Wilson claims that the brutality of the treatment was Henry's responsibility. Other historians might disagree with this and blame men like Cromwell. What evidence would be needed to support Wilson's point of view?

Thomas Cromwell and the encouragement of Protestant ideas

The Reformation in England was driven from the top. Although there was clear evidence of anti-clericalism and discontent with aspects of the Church, it was not a groundswell of public opinion that led to the introduction of reformist doctrine and practices. The changes were often driven by the victors in the factional struggles around the king, although they required the king's support. Between 1535 and 1540, Thomas Cromwell was the force behind the changes.

Cromwell's role as Vicegerent in Spirituals

Cromwell was appointed as Vicegerent in Spirituals in 1535. To place a layman in charge of the direction of religious policy was highly unusual. It seems very likely that Henry did not believe he could entrust the job of restructuring the Church to a prelate, since it was here that his policy was most likely to encounter opposition.

Ten Articles, 1536

The purpose of the Ten Articles was to define the faith and practices of the new national Church in England:

- The sacraments of baptism, penance and the Eucharist were acknowledged, although penance was not fully adopted.

- The real presence of Christ in the Eucharist was reaffirmed.

- The Lutheran doctrine of justification by faith alone was outlined.

> **Source 3**
> (From the Ten Articles, 1536)
>
> Certain faith and hope is gotton and also confirmed, and made more strong by the applying of Christ's words and promises of His grace and favour contained in His gospel.

> **Source 4**
> (From G.W. Bernard, *The King's Reformation: Henry VIII and the Remaking of the English Church*, published by Yale 2005)
>
> What the king attempted was a delicate balancing act; he wanted the pope denounced and his own royal supremacy asserted; he wanted those measures that he was taking to purify the church to be defended; but he wanted no Lutheran or Zwinglian reformation.

Henry wanted to avoid the rebellions caused by Luther's teachings in Germany. His approach was therefore conservative, and Cromwell recognised the necessity for this. Yet there were also significant moves towards a Protestant standpoint in the Ten Articles: there was no mention of the four other Catholic sacraments and great emphasis was placed on the authority of scripture.

Essential notes

The term vicegerent means deputy. It was a position equivalent to papal legate and gave Cromwell authority over both archbishoprics. Henry no doubt chose Cromwell for this job as the most able administrator in his court. Cromwell's influence in parliament would enable him to steer through the necessary legislation. The alternative would have been Thomas Cranmer, but while he was enthusiastic about reform, he was not skilled in the art of politics.

Examiners' notes

Study this extract from the Ten Articles. The word 'apply' is very important here. It suggests that Henry was not prepared to accept *sola fidism* (the belief that salvation was achieved by faith alone) entirely and that he still emphasised the Catholic doctrine of good works being necessary for salvation.

Essential notes

The term Zwinglian refers to the reformer Huldrych Zwingli, who was the leader of the Reformation in Switzerland. The doctrine he developed placed great authority on the Bible and denied the Catholic belief in transubstantiation.

The Bishops' Book, 1537

The Bishops' Book was ordered by Henry in the aftermath of the rebellions (collectively known as the Pilgrimage of Grace – see pages 67–71). In some ways, it was more orthodox than the Ten Articles:

- All seven sacraments were acknowledged, but the four missing from the Ten Articles were said to be of lesser value.

- The need to continue with good works was emphasised.

However, at the same time:

- The mass was deemed to be of less importance.

- The special status of the priest was downgraded.

Henry refused to endorse the book specifically, although he allowed it to be printed. This suggests that while he did not oppose the content, at the same time it did not completely conform to his views.

Cromwell's Injunctions, 1536 and 1538

Cromwell's influence is perhaps most evident in the Injunctions that removed Catholic superstitions and ceremonies from the English Church. They changed religious practices and signalled to the ordinary population that religion was being reformed.

1536 Injunctions	1538 Injunctions
The clergy must defend the Royal Supremacy in sermons	All parishes were to have an English Bible by 1540
Children were to be taught the Lord's Prayer, the Ten Commandments, and other verses from scripture	Pilgrimages were discouraged
The number of Holy Days would be reduced	Candles before images were forbidden
	Relics to be removed from churches
Bibles would be provided in Latin and English for people to read in church	Registration of births, deaths and marriages in parishes

The English Bible, 1538

Cromwell commissioned Miles Coverdale to produce a Great Bible in English. The cover sheet made an important statement about Henry's role as Supreme Head of the Church in England: he was depicted distributing the Word of God to his people, and the figure of God was tiny in comparison.

Henry was concerned that allowing his subjects access to the Bible might lead to debate. Therefore, he ordered that anyone who wished to own a Bible must have a licence. In practice, this restricted Bible reading to the nobility and wealthier gentry.

Cromwell was very enthusiastic about access to the Bible and provided considerable sums of his own money to pay for English Bibles for every parish. He therefore played a key role in driving forward an essential element of Protestantism – access to the Scriptures in the vernacular (mother tongue). People would be able to read and interpret the Bible for themselves for the first time. Cromwell believed that studying the scriptures would remove the influence of Catholic teaching and advance Protestantism.

Examiners' notes

The full title of the Bishops' Book was *Institution of a Christian Man*. It became known as the Bishops' Book because it was produced under the authority of 21 bishops. Cromwell does not appear to have played a role in its production. However, it is essential that you appreciate its importance as evidence of the involvement of leading churchmen in the Reformation. It also shows that views beyond those of Cromwell held sway. The difference in the attitudes of Cromwell and the bishops to the sacraments is made clear: in the Ten Articles, Cromwell only acknowledged three, whereas the bishops accepted all seven.

Examiners' notes

The material on these pages reveals that Cromwell was more enthusiastic for reform than Henry, who was concerned about the chances of rebellion by people who clung to traditional Catholic beliefs and refuted change or, as had occurred in the Peasants' Rebellion in Germany in 1525, would use criticisms of the rich in the Bible to develop their own religious beliefs and justify an attack on the rich.

The impact of factions on the reform of the Church

The process of reform was always going to be difficult. A very conservative clergy and population in many regions necessitated a measured process towards reform. Furthermore, the influence of the opposing factions at court had a very significant impact on policy and determined the extent of success. Cromwell, in particular, had to play a very skillful balancing act to achieve his aims.

The fall of Anne Boleyn, 1536

Anne had played a vital role in initiating the Reformation. However, by 1536 she had fallen out of favour with the king. She also found herself the victim of factional opposition.

The reasons for Anne's fall and execution are summarised below.

The consequences of Catherine of Aragon's death	While Catherine was alive, Henry needed to remain married to Anne to prevent any suggestion that he could return to his first wife. Catherine's death in January 1536 opened up the possibility of an alliance with Charles V, but this would require the restoration of Mary to the succession. Anne would never allow Princess Elizabeth to be declared illegitimate.
The king's doubts on the validity of his marriage	Henry began to voice concerns that his previous relationship with Mary Boleyn invalidated his marriage to Anne. He claimed that the Levitical argument he had used to justify the annulment of his marriage to Catherine (see pages 38 and 42) was similarly valid.
Anne's temperament	Anne's temper was fiery and her behaviour often unpredictable. Anne's enthusiasm for reform conflicted with Henry's belief that women should not interfere in religion.
Anne's failure to produce a son	In June 1534, Anne's second pregnancy ended in stillbirth. Then, in January 1536, she miscarried a 15-week foetus. It was rumoured that the miscarried foetus was deformed. The miscarriage confirmed Henry's doubts about the validity of his marriage.
The anti-Boleyn faction	A new faction headed by Edward Seymour encouraged opposition to Anne. It was joined by Cromwell. Edward hoped to get rid of Anne with his sister Jane, a demure lady-in-waiting who had already caught Henry's eye.
The role of Cromwell	Cromwell had argued with Anne over foreign policy and the control of patronage. Although he had risen as a member of her faction, he was only too prepared to attack Anne and so preserve his own position and the progress of the reformation.

The role of Cromwell (continued)	Cromwell launched an attack on Anne by aligning temporarily with the remaining conservative faction in court. It was his decision that Anne would be removed not on a technicality of canon law, but for treason.
	Members of the king's household, including Sir Henry Norris, Sir Francis Breton and Anne's brother Lord Rochford, were arrested along with Anne's musician Mark Smeaton. The men were accused of committing adultery with the queen.
The accusations against Anne	Cromwell presented Henry with evidence that the queen had committed adultery and incest. In the trial, Cromwell made the charge that Anne and her lovers had plotted to kill the king.
	Only Smeaton, who had been tortured, confessed to the charges.
	Anne was found guilty and beheaded by a French swordsman on 19 May 1536.

The Seymour marriage

Henry married Jane Seymour eleven days after Anne's execution. She was everything that the king wanted in a wife, modest and uninvolved in politics. Most importantly she provided Henry with the long-awaited male heir, Prince Edward, who was born in September 1537. Jane died twelve days after the birth as a result of complications and poor care.

Jane's role in the Reformation was therefore extremely limited. However, the marriage itself was important because it led to the promotion in the court of Edward Seymour, who became Earl of Hertford shortly after Edward's birth. He was an enthusiastic supporter of reform and so gave additional support to Cromwell's drive for religious change. He became a leading member of the reformist faction that promoted religious change.

The rise of the reformist faction and its influence

The removal of Anne Boleyn significantly increased Cromwell's powers in the Privy Chamber. David Starkey has suggested that Anne played the role of chief minister at times, and that her existence was therefore often unwelcome competition to Cromwell:

- Cromwell grasped the opportunity to fill the vacant places created by the purge of Henry's gentlemen during the investigation into Anne's adultery with his own followers. Men like Anthony Denny and Ralph Sadler were convinced evangelicals who in turn used their influence over patronage to promote other reformers to the court.

- These promotions enhanced Cromwell's power in the court and enabled him to pursue the foreign policy that Anne had opposed: a Protestant alliance in Europe to protect England from the threat of Catholic invasion.

- In 1539, Cromwell finally secured Henry's agreement to a marriage to Anne of Cleves, sister to the Duke of Cleves, Protestant ruler of an important imperial duchy that would deter Charles V from planning an attack on England.

- Cromwell was optimistic that this marriage would also secure the continued programme of reform.

Essential notes

Little credence can be given to the 21 specified charges. As Eric Ives says, 'quadruple adultery plus incest invites disbelief'. Anne was not even present at the location stated on at least 12 of them.

Essential notes

Cromwell's promotions in the court are very noteworthy. These men came from gentry backgrounds and would not in normal circumstances have been expected to rise so high. Denny became Chief Gentleman in 1538. This shows clear evidence of the nature of a changing court, and it is not surprising that members of the nobility resented Cromwell for his promotions, which favoured ability over rank.

Essential notes

The term monastery was not in general use in the 16th century. Contemporary sources refer to abbeys, nunneries, and small houses called friaries.

The dissolution of the monasteries: Causes and process

One of the most significant religious changes in this period was the dissolution of the monasteries. It was perhaps here that the impact of Henry's reformation was felt most obviously by the English people.

England in 1535 was a land populated with monasteries. There were more than 800 of them and they performed a range of services:

- praying for the souls of the dead
- healing the sick
- providing charity for the poor
- educating the young
- employing labourers on the land.

The religious importance of the monasteries and the impact of Protestant ideas

Monasteries had an essential role to play in the Catholic faith. It was necessary for prayers to be said to aid the release of souls from purgatory. The monks performed this function.

Essential notes

Henry VII had paid for 10 000 masses to be said by the monks for his soul after he died. This is an example of a common practice in the Catholic Church – people bequeathed money and property to monasteries for the monks to pray for them.

However, Protestants argued that there was no biblical evidence of purgatory. Also, since in their view salvation was achieved by faith alone, there was no need for monks to pray for the dead and so monasteries had no role in the new Church.

Monks were also a threat to the Royal Supremacy because many of them were reluctant to accept the authority of the king instead of the Pope.

Stage 1: *Valor Ecclesiasticus*, 1535
The initial stage in the dissolution of the monasteries was the compilation of reports on the state of the monasteries.

- In 1535, Cromwell despatched a set of commissioners to investigate the wealth of the Church.
- The results were recorded in a document called *Valor Ecclesiasticus* (the Latin for 'church valuation').
- This report revealed tremendous wealth held by the monastic houses. Monastic income was three times greater than the revenues generated by Crown lands. This was a powerful incentive for the king to take possession of the monastic lands.

Examiners' notes

When using Source 5 to reach a judgement, you need to examine beyond the surface features – it was produced by Layton, one of Cromwell's visitors, who was sent out specifically to find corruption. You need to consider whether Layton's findings were exaggerated or representative of monastic life as a whole.

Stage 2: The visitations, 1535
Cromwell then sent out a second set of commissioners to investigate the standards in the monasteries. The visitations were not conducted by impartial agents – Cromwell had instructed them to find corruption and to report on it.

The reports would justify intervention by the king: as Head of the Church in England, it was his responsibility to reform it.

Although many houses were reported to be in good order, many tales of the type of immorality outlined in Source 5 were received by Cromwell.

Source 5
(From Richard Layton's report on Syon Abbey, 1535)

The Bishop persuaded one of his lay brethren, a smith, to have made a key for the door, to have in the night-time received in wenches for him and his fellow and especially a wife of Uxbridge. The said Bishop also persuaded a nun, to whom he was confessor, to submit her body to his pleasure, and thus he persuaded her in confession, if she were immediately after confessed by him, and took of him absolution, she should be clear forgiven of God...

Stage 3: Act for the dissolution of the smaller monasteries, 1536

- The visitors' evidence was placed before parliament in 1536.

- Cromwell drew up a bill that declared the smaller monastic houses worth less than £200 annually should be closed immediately because of their corruption.

Source 6
(Adapted from the Act for the Dissolution of the Smaller Monasteries, 1536)

There can be no reformation of this problem [corruption] unless such small houses are utterly suppressed and the religious persons in them committed to great and honourable monasteries, where they may be compelled to live religiously for reformation of their lives.

Stage 4: The process of dissolution

This began immediately.

- Abbeys were plundered, the monks and nuns turned out into the countryside.

- Medieval artwork was destroyed or taken off into private possession and roofs were stripped of their lead.

About 500 religious houses were dissolved, and the wealth this generated was brought to the newly formed Court of Augmentations.

Stage 5: The second dissolution Act, 1539

The announcement in 1536 that larger monastic houses were free from corruption gave the impression that Henry was reforming not destroying. Later, he could claim that it was necessary to close the larger houses in response to their role in the rebellions of 1536, when they opposed royal authority and acted in a treasonous manner. However, this argument is not entirely convincing.

The dissolution of the monasteries was extremely lucrative for a king who was short of money, and the continued existence of the abbeys could not be condoned when their religious purpose had vanished. In fact, pressure from Cromwell had led to most monastic houses 'voluntarily' dissolving themselves. Thus, the second Act of 1539 was recognising an accomplished fact – the monasteries had been dissolved.

Examiners' notes

There is clear evidence of sexual misconduct in Source 5. The fact that it was attributed to a bishop who then encouraged the same behaviour in other monks and nuns suggests an institutionalised corruption that had permeated the whole Church, rather than this being the misdeeds of a single individual.

Essential notes

There was already a precedent for closing small houses; Wolsey had closed 30 abbeys that were not viable and had taken their wealth to fund his college at Oxford. Therefore this measure could be justified as necessary for reform.

Essential notes

Cromwell set up the Court of Augmentations to collect the vast sums of money that were generated by the dissolution of the monasteries, including the sale of properties and the rents.

Support for the dissolution of the monasteries

Although the process of dissolution resulted in the most dangerous rebellion of Henry's reign (the Pilgrimage of Grace) there were reasons why many individuals supported the policy of dissolution.

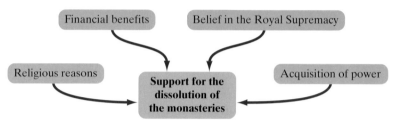

Reasons for supporting the dissolution of the monasteries

The king's motives

- According to G.W. Bernard, Henry had never had much commitment to the monasteries. He had not been an enthusiastic participant in pilgrimages and his offerings to monasteries had been only what convention expected. Therefore, Bernard suggests, he had no enthusiasm for the role of the monasteries and hence no reason to spare them.

- Henry's income had always been too small for his expenses and especially for him to realise his foreign policy ambitions. Even though Cromwell was very skilled in persuading Henry to avoid the expensive foreign adventures of the 1520s, the consequences of his annulment had made England vulnerable to a Catholic attack from the continent, and Henry therefore needed funds to improve the nation's defences.

- *Valor Ecclesiasticus* had revealed the vast wealth of the Church. As Head of the Church in England, this was Henry's wealth. Acquisition of such wealth potentially freed him from the restrictions of requesting taxes from parliament. One key factor driving Henry's support for dissolution was therefore the financial benefits it would bring.

- In addition, the monks had been among the most vocal opponents to the break with Rome and the establishment of the Royal Supremacy; dissolution would remove that opposition.

Financial benefits for the gentry and nobility

The wealth acquired by the king through dissolution significantly expanded his capacity to grant patronage to his closest supporters. This, in turn, enabled them to extend patronage to their clients. Cromwell, for example, gained very generous livings from the dissolution.

Source 7
(From Robert Hutchinson, *Thomas Cromwell*, published by Phoenix 2008)

In February 1538 Henry granted Lewes Priory and its proceeds to his Minister. Cromwell was anxious to speedily destroy the Cluniac priory and provide a new, grand house at Lewes for the enjoyment of his son Gregory, worthy of his family's status.

The possibility of amassing great wealth explains why even those who were conservative in religion were inclined to support the dissolution. A prime example is the Duke of Norfolk:

Source 8
(From Robert Hutchinson, *House of Treason: The Rise and Fall of a Tudor Dynasty*, published by Weidenfeld & Nicolson 2009)

Norfolk was in the vanguard of the unseemly scramble for monastic riches. Even in the diverse morality of Tudor England, how could the devout and religiously conservative Norfolk enrich himself on the proceeds of the dissolved monasteries? The answer is twofold: firstly he was always driven by a need for ever greater power and status. Secondly, on the political front, the duke was a firm believer in authority; if suppression of the monasteries was Henry's policy, so be it.

Belief in the Royal Supremacy

A belief in the Royal Supremacy was an essential ingredient in the acceptance and support of Henry's policy. For many who would not benefit from the spoils of the monasteries, support for the dissolution stemmed from obedience to their king. This submission was enforced by the oaths that Henry required the nobility and gentry to take.

Support for religious reasons

Reformers wholeheartedly supported the dissolution. Rejection of the Catholic belief in purgatory meant the monasteries had no religious purpose, while many Catholic Reformers, following the teachings of Erasmus, believed that monasteries were redundant and so did not defend them in the face of attack.

Source 9
(From the Act of 1536 dissolving monasteries with an income of less than £200 a year)

Manifest sin, vicious, carnal and abominable living is being daily used and committed among the small abbeys, priories and other religious houses . . . unless such small houses are utterly suppressed there can be no reform of these matters.

For the members of parliament who voted in favour of this Act and the reformist population they represented, religious zeal was a driving force in their support for the dissolution. Their expectation was that the policy would shortly be extended to the larger houses, as indeed it was in 1539.

Examiners' notes

Hutchinson raises an interesting point. Norfolk's religious beliefs were Catholic. He accepted the Royal Supremacy, but as the finishing point not the starting point of reform. He would be expected to oppose dissolution, but the lure of wealth outstripped his faith. Hutchinson develops a key reason why conservative members of the nobility supported dissolution: obedience to the monarch.

Essential notes

English subjects had been brought up to believe that the monarch had the right to direct policy. In some cases, this show of loyalty was genuine; in other cases, it was forced in order that punishment could be avoided.

Essential notes

Desiderius Erasmus was a Dutch Catholic priest who was an early promoter of reform in the Catholic Church.

Examiners' notes

Source 9 emphasises that the motive was reform. Edward Hall notes that in this sitting of parliament, at least one MP said that there could be no reform unless the large abbeys were dissolved too. Therefore, in 1536, there was already a drive to dissolve all the monasteries that had not come only from the king or Cromwell.

Opposition to the dissolution of the monasteries, 1536–37

Although the majority of the population accepted Henry's religious changes, including the dissolution of the monasteries, the policy led to the biggest rebellion of Henry's reign when 30 000 people in the north rose up in revolt.

The Lincolnshire rebellion, 1536

The trigger for the rebellion was the activity of three government commissions working in the county focused on the following tasks:

- dissolving the smaller monasteries

- collecting the Subsidy granted by parliament in 1534

- inspecting the quality of the clergy.

The tensions already present boiled over when a rumour began circulating that the commissioners were intending to strip the churches of gold, jewels and plate, and to extract extra taxes.

Timeline of events

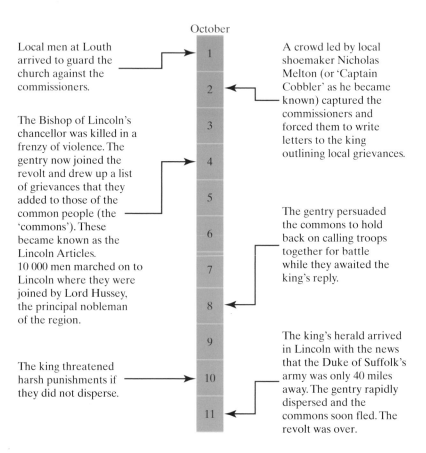

October

Local men at Louth arrived to guard the church against the commissioners.

1

2

A crowd led by local shoemaker Nicholas Melton (or 'Captain Cobbler' as he became known) captured the commissioners and forced them to write letters to the king outlining local grievances.

3

The Bishop of Lincoln's chancellor was killed in a frenzy of violence. The gentry now joined the revolt and drew up a list of grievances that they added to those of the common people (the 'commons'). These became known as the Lincoln Articles. 10 000 men marched on to Lincoln where they were joined by Lord Hussey, the principal nobleman of the region.

4

5

6

The gentry persuaded the commons to hold back on calling troops together for battle while they awaited the king's reply.

7

8

9

The king threatened harsh punishments if they did not disperse.

10

The king's herald arrived in Lincoln with the news that the Duke of Suffolk's army was only 40 miles away. The gentry rapidly dispersed and the commons soon fled. The revolt was over.

11

The king ordered over a hundred death sentences, but in the end only 57 were carried out.

The Pilgrimage of Grace, 1536

Henry's troubles were not over: a greater danger was brewing in Yorkshire, which exploded into full scale revolt by 10 October.

Source 10
(From Edward Hall's account of the Pilgrimage of Grace, November 1536)

They declared, by their proclamation solemnly made, that their insurrection should extend no further than to the maintenance and defence of the faith of Christ and the deliverance of holy church, sore decayed and oppressed. They called this a holy and blessed pilgrimage; they also had certain banners in the field whereon was painted Christ hanging on the cross on one side, and a chalice with a painted cake in it on the other side.

Events

- By October 10, Robert Aske had become the leader of the Pilgrims, as they called themselves. The numbers swelled to 30 000.

- All men were made to take an oath to defend the Church and be loyal to the king.

- They marched under the banner of the Five Wounds of Christ from York to Pontefract Castle, an important strategic fortress that guarded the road to London. Lord Darcy, who held the castle, handed it over to the rebels.

Source 11
(From Anthony Fletcher and Diarmaid MacCulloch, *Tudor Rebellions*, published by Longman 2008)

Darcy pretended at first that he was opposed to the rising. Yet he surrendered Pontefract extraordinarily quickly. Moreover, when he did so he was ready to distribute to the rebels numerous badges of the Five Wounds, which had presumably been stored in his castle since his retinue wore them on an expedition against the Moors in Spain more than twenty years before.

The rebels were also aided by the Percy family of Northumberland. Sir Thomas Percy, brother of the Earl of Northumberland, led a force of 600 rebels to join the forces attacking the abbey at Jervaulx.

The pilgrims now had control of the north of England. They drew up a list of grievances to present to the king, known as the Pontefract Articles, and began restoring monasteries that had been dissolved.

The population of England in Henry's reign was 2.75 million, so the 30 000 rebels in the Pilgrimage of Grace were a significant minority. The numbers would not have been so threatening if they had been scattered around the country, but they were concentrated in Yorkshire and made a sizeable army more than three times larger than the king's.

Examiners' notes

This source is useful to examine for opinion. Here, Hall presents the reasons given by the pilgrims for their rebellion, yet careful study reveals Hall's own opinion. His description of the Eucharist on the pilgrims' banner of the Five Wounds of Christ as painted cake clearly shows that he rejected the doctrine of transubstantiation and was not sympathetic to their cause.

Essential notes

Robert Aske was the younger son of a gentry family from Howden, East Yorkshire. He had a legal practice in York and so had contacts with the northern gentry and nobility.

Essential notes

The north had always been a difficult part of the kingdom to rule. In 1530 Henry revived the Council of the North to bring the region under control.

Reasons for and responses to the Pilgrimage of Grace

Causes of the uprising

The diagram below summarises the reasons for the uprising that became known as the Pilgrimage of Grace. The diagram makes it clear that there were multiple causes of the rebellion. Many historians, using evidence such as that presented on the next page, regard the religious causes as the most important motivating factors.

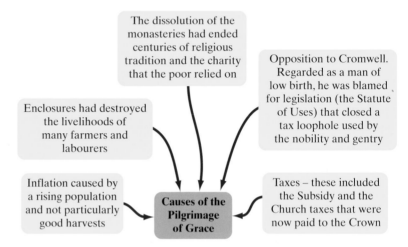

The causes of the Pilgrimage of Grace

The Pilgrimage of Grace challenged Henry's authority and suggested that it was under significant threat. The opposition to the dissolution of the monasteries directly challenged the Royal Supremacy. If Henry could not quell the rebellion, his decision to enact religious changes would be overturned by the rebels. In this way, his power would be seriously undermined.

Henry could not be seen to tolerate this or to back down.

The king's response to the rebellion

Initially, Henry appeared to be willing to negotiate. The royal forces led by the Duke of Norfolk numbered just 8000, which was considerably less than the 30 000 under Aske's command.

Norfolk met with Aske and an agreement was reached:

- The rebels would be granted a general pardon.

- A parliament would be held at York to discuss the grievances.

- No more monasteries would be suppressed before the parliament met.

Aske was invited down to court for Christmas. He was further encouraged to sell this deal to the pilgrims, who began to disperse.

The pilgrims may have been fooled into thinking that the king would address their grievances, but they had been duped by Norfolk, who had been instructed to make promises in order to get them to disband.

Norfolk's intention to disperse the rebels by making them false promises is made clear in this letter he sent to Henry:

Source 12
(From a letter from the Duke of Norfolk to Henry VIII, 27 October 1536)

Whatever happen I shall not spare the little poor carcass. I beg you take in good part whatever (at the advice of others) I may promise the rebels; for surely I shall observe no part thereof, for any respect of that other might call mine honour stained, longer than I and my company may be assembled together; for I think no promise made to serve you can stain me, who would rather be torn to pieces than show cowardice or disloyalty.

Source 13
(From G.W. Bernard, *The King's Reformation: Henry VIII and the Remaking of the English Church*, published by Yale 2005)

Henry had disguised his true sentiments to Aske and he was always determined that he would prevail. He insisted on the evil of rebellion. He insisted that the gentry should make submission and receive the king's mercy. He was imposing an oath that would compel the northern gentry openly to renounce the rebellion. He wanted the instigators of the rebellion to be searched out even though he had pardoned them for any offences they had committed.

Henry kept none of the promises made. His opportunity came in January 1537 when Sir Francis Bigod, frustrated by the slow progress, led a rising. He planned to capture Hull and Scarborough and force Norfolk to make good on his promises. However, he had little support now that the pilgrims had returned home and he fled to Cumberland where he was captured within a few days.

Henry now proceeded without mercy:

- 178 rebels were executed.
- Lord Darcy was beheaded on Tower Hill.
- Lord Hussey was beheaded in Lincoln.
- Robert Aske was hanged outside Clifford's Tower in York.
- The Percy family were forced to name Henry as the heir to the Northumberland estates.

Henry and Cromwell proceeded with the dissolution of the monasteries, justifying the measure as necessary to stamp out treason.

Examiners' notes

Compare these two sources that focus on the government's response to the rebellion. The letter from Norfolk emphasises the loyalty of the duke in particular and allows us to draw inferences about the support of the nobility in general for the Crown's policy. Norfolk is seeking assurances that Henry will not read treachery into his actions taken to disperse the rebels. The second source emphasises the king's personal role in ending the rebellion. Bernard makes a clear argument that Henry was responsible for the suppression of the rebellion. Norfolk had made promises that neither he nor Henry ever intended to keep. Note Bernard's constant use of phrases such as 'he insisted' and 'he wanted' to emphasise Henry's personal role.

The failure of resistance

Why the rebellions failed

The events outlined on pages 67–69 and Henry's reaction to them provides some clear evidence of why the rebellion was unsuccessful and why Henry was able to suppress it.

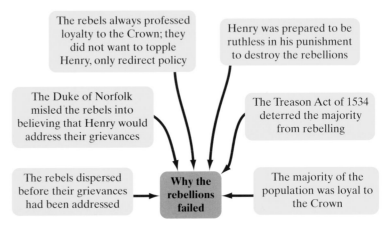

Reasons for the suppression of the rebellions

Outcome of the rebellion

The destruction of the Pilgrimage of Grace ended any serious opposition to the Crown during Henry's reign:

- Henry's retribution had been absolute and this made an important impression on the population. His readiness to enact the death penalty ensured that most potential rebels kept their criticisms to themselves; treason could be spoken as well as acted on.

- It is also important to note that the overwhelming majority of the population remained loyal to the Crown. Even the rebels had declared this, as Source 14 shows.

Essential notes

One reason why opposition was stamped out was the use of the Treason Act of 1534. Although the rebels claimed to support the king, it was inescapable that their actions denied this.

Examiners' notes

Study Source 14 carefully. The reference to 'common blood and bad counsel' is undoubtedly aimed at Cromwell, but it is clear that loyalty to the king was a key element. The rebels claimed to be rebelling for the king, not against him.

Source 14
(From the Oath of the Honourable Men, devised by Robert Aske to be taken by all those following the Pilgrimage of Grace in 1536)

Ye shall not join this, our Pilgrimage of Grace, except for the love you bear to Almighty God and to the maintenance of the Holy Church, the safety of the King and his children, to the purifying of the nobility and the removal of those of common blood and bad counsel from his advisers.

While the rebels opposed the powers of Cromwell, they did not deny the rights of the king. Within the population as a whole, some groups welcomed the introduction of Protestantism. For others, the claim that the king was divinely ordained was accepted and therefore his decisions regarding religion were respected.

It should be noted that the rebellion took place in the north although there was sympathy for it elsewhere. According to Christopher Haigh:

> **Source 15**
> (From Christopher Haigh, *English Reformations: Religion, politics, and society under the Tudors*, published by Clarendon Press 1993)
>
> There was widespread sympathy in southern counties for the Pilgrim cause. At Windsor a priest tried to persuade those mustering for the royal army that any who joined the northern cause "did fight and defend God's quarrel".

Haigh does not recount how successful the priest was in making his plea, and it seems to be the case that open rebellion in large numbers was limited to the north. Loyalty to the Crown appears to have been the attitude of the majority.

It is also worth noting that Haigh raises an important point in this extract about southern sympathy. Although it is often claimed that the people in the south were anti-clerical and more receptive to Protestant ideas, this is too sweeping a statement to apply to the whole southern population. The example here is one of a number that Haigh lists, including disturbances in Walsingham and Cornwall. In this way he demonstrates that opposition in the south was scattered and lacked the coordination of the rebellion in the north.

Evaluating the extent of resistance
The information in this table suggests that on balance effective deterrents limited the amount of resistance that Henry had to face.

Resistance posed a serious threat	There was a limited threat from resistance
The rebels in the Pilgrimage of Grace had supporters from the nobility including Lords Darcy and Hussey	The Pilgrimage of Grace was confined to Yorkshire
The rebels appealed to Charles V for help	The population at large and the rebels professed loyalty to the king
30 000 people joined the rebellion whilst Henry had an army of just 8000	The Treason Act of 1534 stamped out most potential opposition
There was some sympathy for the rebels in the south	Henry's punishments, including his readiness to enact the death penalty, ensured that potential rebels kept their criticism to themselves; treason could be spoken as well as acted on.

Examiners' notes

Remember that the Pilgrimage of Grace was not the only manifestation of opposition to religious change. Consider opposition from court factions (pages 54–55, 72), key figures of opposition (pages 56–57), opposition from monasteries themselves (pages 62–63) and other rebellions (page 66).

Examiners' notes

When evaluating the severity of the threat of resistance you could consider issues such as the piecemeal nature of religious change.

The retreat from reform

Henry was naturally inclined towards orthodoxy in religion. While he
would never again countenance the Pope as Head of the Church and he
was determined to take control of the Church's wealth, he had a preference
for the ceremonies, symbols and prayers of his childhood.

Henry's enthusiasm for reforming the doctrine and practices of the Church
was never as great as was Cromwell's, and the rebellions of 1536–37 served
as a reminder that rapid religious change caused social and political unrest
and was dangerous to him.

Therefore, in the latter years in the 1530s, Henry began to limit the pace of
reformation and stepped in to define the doctrine along traditional lines
that would be acceptable to all. The rebellions of 1536–7 no doubt played a
role in the timing of the king's decision to steer the religion along a more
orthodox path. Thus the opposition combined with Henry's inclinations
meant that the years after 1537 would be characterised by a retreat from
certain aspects of reform.

The rise of the conservative faction

The conservative faction was defined by its belief that the Royal Supremacy
was the end point of reform, not the beginning. The leading members of
the faction were:

- Thomas Howard, Duke of Norfolk, the foremost peer of the realm

- Stephen Gardiner, the Bishop of Winchester.

By 1539, they had gained increasing influence over Henry, which they used
to criticise his chief minister and encourage a return to orthodoxy.

Howard and Gardiner are often credited with bringing a halt to reform by
encouraging the introduction of the Act of Six Articles.

Act of Six Articles, 1539

The Act of Six Articles, passed in June 1539, is often seen as a key sign that
Henry rejected Protestant reform.

The Act confirmed	The Act banned
The king was the Supreme Head of the Church	Marriage of priests
Transubstantiation	Marriage of anyone who had taken vows of chastity
Private mass	The taking of communion in both kinds (bread and wine) by the laity
The hearing of confession by priests	

How far was the Act a retreat from reform?

The following diagram reveals the differences between Cromwell's statement
of faith in the Ten Articles of 1536 and Henry's Act of Six Articles of 1539.

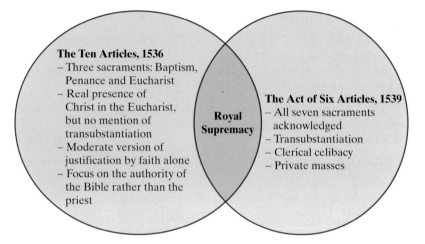

Differences between the Ten Articles (1536) and the Act of Six Articles (1539)

The diagram indicates that there was a greater emphasis on traditional faith, but it would be difficult to argue that the Six Articles restored an essentially Catholic doctrine:

- The pre-eminence of the Royal Supremacy undermines any argument that Henry was Catholic.

- It is also important to remember that, in the same year as this Act was passed, Henry proceeded with the dissolution of the larger monasteries, which was a clear attack on Catholic beliefs and practices.

What was the purpose of the Act?

G.R Elton is of the opinion that the Six Articles embodied full Catholic doctrine and could have been used as a decisive weapon against the Protestants whose reforms had been rejected. However, this version tends to suggest that Henry did not know his own mind and that religious policy was in the hands of the factions. This view is rejected by G.W Bernard:

> ### Source 16
> (From G.W Bernard, *The King's Reformation: Henry VIII and the Remaking of the English Church*, published by Yale 2005)
>
> It is a mistake to see the Six Articles of 1539 as in any important sense a reversal of royal policy. Nothing in the Six Articles contradicted Henry's previous aims. It is essential to grasp that the act was not a comprehensive statement, let alone a revision, of doctrine. Its purpose was to pronounce on key matters of doctrine and practice that were coming into dispute, with the aim of halting damaging current controversies.

Bernard puts the king firmly in control of policy. He argues that Henry took a leading role in drawing up the Articles with the intention of curbing a dangerous diversity in religion that threatened the realm's stability.

Essential notes

Current historical opinion is that Henry was seeking a middle way in religion that would be accepted by the whole community, and that this would remove opposition and so any threats to the Crown.

There were severe penalties for anyone who went against the Act. Indeed, anyone who denied transubstantiation was automatically subject to burning.

Examiners' notes

According to Bernard, the Six Articles was not the result of factional victory on behalf of the conservatives, but Henry's policy. Both the reformer Cromwell and the conservative Gardiner played their part in steering the legislation through parliament.

The fall of Thomas Cromwell, 1538–40

Cromwell served Henry loyally and well for more than eight years, six as his undeniable chief minister. However, he was not popular with the nobility and higher gentry in the court; his low origins offended them and he was regarded as monopolising power.

By 1538, the tide was beginning to turn against Cromwell. In 1540, he was overwhelmed by the opposition, found guilty of treason and heresy, and executed.

The trial of John Lambert

The trial of the reformer John Lambert is taken as a sign that Henry was concerned that Cromwell's reforms were leading to the spread of heresy:

- Cromwell set up the trial over which Henry himself presided.

- Lambert's fate was decided when he denied the real presence of Christ in the Eucharist.

- Henry pronounced him guilty.

- Cromwell, however, had appeared to give Lambert the benefit of the doubt in the trial. This raised questions about Cromwell's own beliefs that his enemies would later use against him.

The significance of the Act of Six Articles

The Act of Six Articles may not have marked a rejection of reform, but it did show that Henry was conservative rather than radical in religion. This inspired the conservative faction to increase their attacks on Cromwell, perceiving that they had discovered the minister's vulnerable spot.

Hans Holbein's painting of Anne of Cleves, circa 1539

The Cleves marriage and its failure

The interlinking of Cromwell's foreign and domestic policy also ran into problems by 1540:

- The possibility of a Catholic attack on England encouraged Cromwell to search for an alliance, which he forged with the Duchy of Cleves.

- The alliance would be sealed by a marriage between Henry and Anne, sister of the Duke of Cleves.

- Henry declared himself impressed by Holbein's painting of Anne, and Cromwell proceeded to organise the marriage.

- However, when Anne arrived, Henry claimed that she was a 'fat Flanders mare' who did not look like her painting.

Cromwell persuaded Henry to go through with the marriage for the sake of the alliance, but Henry did not consummate the marriage and he blamed Cromwell for 'forcing' him into it. He claimed that Anne was no maid and that a pre-contracted betrothal to the Duke of Lorraine invalidated their marriage.

The changing situation in Europe

One of the underlying factors that led to Cromwell's fall was the changing foreign situation.

In 1539, there was a respite in the Hapsburg–Valois conflict, and the accord between Charles V and Francis I raised the prospect of them launching a Catholic crusade against England with the sanction of the Pope. This prompted Cromwell's furious marriage preparations.

However, by mid-1540, the two European monarchs were at loggerheads once more and the Protestant alliance was no longer necessary. This increased Henry's dissatisfaction with his chief minister.

The rise of the Howard faction and the role of Catherine Howard

The conservative faction had long been looking for a way to bring Cromwell down, and the perfect opportunity now arose. The Duke of Norfolk brought his niece Catherine Howard to court and the king was soon infatuated with her.

Norfolk was delighted to find that the king wanted to marry his niece. The only obstacle was Cromwell and the Cleves marriage.

Accusations of heresy

Cromwell's fate was probably sealed when his support for a number of heretics came to light:

- Lord Lisle reported that Cromwell had not enforced punishments for heretical behaviour in Calais.
- Robert Barnes, a Lutheran and friend of Cromwell, preached a sermon on justification by faith alone and was sent to the Tower.

This information was used by Norfolk and Bishop Gardiner to bring Cromwell down.

The downfall and execution of Cromwell

Cromwell was arrested at the Council meeting on 10 June 1540. He was tried at the House of Lords by an Act of Attainder which stated:

> **Source 17**
> (From the Act of Attainder against Thomas Cromwell, 29 June 1540)
>
> Thomas Cromwell, contrary to the trust and confidence that your Majesty had in him, caused many of your Majesty's faithful subjects to be greatly influenced by heresies and other errors, contrary to the right laws and pleasure of Almighty God. And in the last day of March 1539 when certain new preachers, such as Robert Barnes, were committed to the Tower of London for preaching and teaching against your Highness's proclamations, Thomas Cromwell confirmed the preacher to be good. And moreover, the said Thomas Cromwell, being a man of very base and low degree, has held the nobles of your realm in great disdain, derision and detestation.

Cromwell was found guilty and executed on 28 July 1540. The executioner botched the execution; it seems he was chosen because of his inexperience. One contemporary account describes the executioner chopping at Cromwell's head and neck for half an hour.

On the same day, Henry married Catherine Howard, his marriage to Anne of Cleves having been annulled.

Essential notes

An Act of Attainder was a medieval device for finding advisers guilty of treason without allowing them to put up a defence. It was necessary to use this against Cromwell since evidence that he had committed treason would be extremely hard to find.

Examiners' notes

Study Source 17. It outlines a wide range of reasons why Cromwell was removed. In question (b) you would be able to develop each reason from your contextual knowledge as the basis for weighing up why Cromwell fell from power. You will need to consider the weight that can be attached to this source, which was drawn up by Cromwell's enemies.

Cromwell's achievements as Henry's Chief Minister

Cromwell was not replaced after his execution. This may imply that Henry realised he had made a mistake in removing his most able administrator. Alternatively, it could be argued that as Henry got older and no longer played sports, he had more time to involve himself in the affairs of government. So the removal of Cromwell provided Henry with the opportunity to take control.

The following balance sheets outline the significant achievements for which Cromwell was responsible and that benefited Henry.

The Royal Supremacy

Achievements	Annulment of Henry's marriage to Catherine
	Control over the clergy (they no longer served two masters)
	Huge extension of royal authority across the whole realm secured by oaths
	Established England as an independent nation state answerable to no other power
	Huge increase in wealth from the dissolved monasteries, sufficient to make Henry financially independent of Parliament and so increase his authority
Difficulties, failures and threats	Excommunication of Henry in December 1538
	Threat of invasion by Catholic monarchs Charles V and Francis I

Finance and administration

Achievements	The Act in Restraint of Annates cut off payments from bishops to the Pope and transferred them to Henry.
	The Act of Dispensations, steered through Parliament by Cromwell, transferred the payments of Peter's Pence to Henry instead of the Pope
	The wealth of the dissolved monasteries (three times that of the Crown lands) now came to Henry.
	Cromwell established the Court of First Fruits and Tenths and the Court of Augmentations to manage all the revenues coming in from the Church
	Cromwell's management of finances was more efficient than they had been under Wolsey. Modern methods of accounting and collecting finances were employed. The courts administered the revenues instead of money being transferred to the Privy Chamber and distributed at the whim of the king
Difficulties, failures and threats	The international threat and Henry's desire to achieve glory by military conquest meant that in the 1540s he rapidly spent the income from the monasteries and left a bankrupt monarchy to his heir

Control across the realm

One of Cromwell's most important contributions was to ensure that Henry's authority extended to the furthest parts of the realm. By doing this, Cromwell assisted in the creation of a unitary state.

Achievements	System of JPs extended to Wales in 1536
	Wales granted the right to return MPs to Parliament, 1536
	The estates held by the Duke of Northumberland were transferred to the Crown when the Duke died in 1537
	A Council of the North under the Bishop of Durham was established in 1537 to bring the north more firmly under the king's control
Difficulties, failures and threats	Rebellions in Lincolnshire and Yorkshire: the Pilgrimage of Grace, 1536–37
	Protestants in Calais flouted the king's policy on religion

Relationship with European powers

A key factor in Wolsey's fall from power was the failure of his foreign policy. Cromwell aimed to make England an independent nation state that was not dependent on or answerable to any outside power. For this policy to succeed, it was vital that Henry did not pursue a foreign policy that required invasion and conquest as a measure of success.

Achievements	Henry was not involved in any wars during Cromwell's period in office
	Improved relations with the Emperor Charles V after 1536
	Establishment of the Protestant alliance in 1539
Difficulties, failures and threats	Threatened invasion by Charles V and Francis I in 1538
	Failure of the Cleves marriage and the Protestant alliance, 1540

Examiners' notes

Study the balance sheet on the Royal Supremacy and finances. Note the interaction between power and money. Cromwell sought to make the Crown strong and stable. Henry's decision to pursue an adventurous foreign policy undermined Cromwell's work by spending all the additional revenues acquired and making the king once more dependent on Parliament for money.

Cromwell achieved his aim of keeping Henry out of war. After Cromwell's death, Henry went to war with both Scotland and France in the 1540s, spending the entire revenues generated by the dissolution in the process.

Conclusion

The balance sheet of Cromwell's achievements is testimony to his considerable skills as a royal servant:

- He significantly enriched the Crown, as well as enhancing Henry's powers, with the Royal Supremacy.
- He extended royal control across the realm through the development of local government.
- He succeeded in keeping Henry out of expensive wars.

This is not to suggest that Cromwell did not face problems or that he was successful in all his activities. For example, his attempt to secure a Protestant alliance through the Cleves marriage turned into a political and personal disaster, while his apparent support for radical Protestant reform left him open to accusations of heresy. However, the problems he faced were not always of his making, and where possible he always worked towards a solution.

Examiners' notes

These pages provide some useful ideas on the motivation for religious change. It also suggests how the conflict between religion and politics played a role in driving the changes.

Was the English Reformation political or religious?

The question of what motivated Henry to bring about changes in the Church is hotly debated by historians. The evidence is ambiguous, as indicated by the diagrams on these pages.

Political motivation

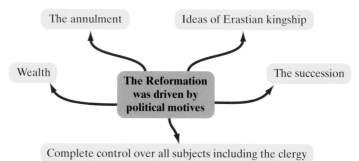

Political motivation for the Reformation

There is little doubt that the initial motivation for the Reformation was political: Henry was insistent on achieving his annulment, and by 1532 it was clear that this could not be achieved while he remained a member of the Catholic Church.

Sources 18 and 19 emphasise the political advantages of removing the authority of the Pope in England. The Royal Supremacy brought all Henry's subjects under his authority and so extended the power of the monarchy.

Examiners' notes

These sources place great emphasis on the importance of subjects, both lay and ecclesiastical, submitting to the authority of the monarch. In this way, they imply that Henry could not rule effectively as long as the clergy answered to the Pope.

They are useful sources to compare for similarities on the question of political motivations.

Source 18
(From the Commons' Supplication against the Ordinaries, drafted by Thomas Cromwell in 1529 and presented to the King in 1532)

The clergy of this realm have made and daily make laws in their Convocation concerning non-spiritual matters. They declare that those who infringe them are subject to excommunication and even guilty of heresy. These laws do not have your assent, and some clash with the laws of your kingdom. They are not even published in English. And by these means your subjects are brought to question your laws and authority and do not know whom to obey.

Source 19
(From A.G.R. Smith, *The Emergence of a Nation State, 1529–1660*, published by Longman 1997)

Guided by Thomas Cromwell, the changes of the 1530s led to the formal establishment of an English 'nation state', a kingdom and people subject to no outside authority.

Religious motivation

The argument that the Henrician Reformation was politically motivated does not provide a sufficient explanation as to why the Reformation did not end once Henry had achieved his annulment.

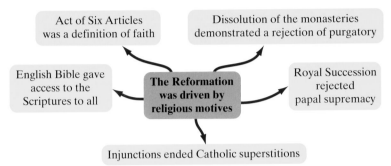

Act of Six Articles was a definition of faith

Dissolution of the monasteries demonstrated a rejection of purgatory

English Bible gave access to the Scriptures to all

The Reformation was driven by religious motives

Royal Succession rejected papal supremacy

Injunctions ended Catholic superstitions

Religious motivation for the Reformation

The diagram above makes it clear that the English Reformation went well beyond the king's initial desire to end his marriage to Catherine of Aragon and marry Anne Boleyn:

- Henry never deviated in his assertion of the Royal Supremacy once it had been declared.

- His choice of reformers – Cromwell and Cranmer – established how Henry intended the Reformation to progress. While he was never as radical in religion as these two men, it would be a mistake to argue that they alone were responsible for the changes to doctrine and practice that characterise the Reformation from 1536.

Source 20
(From G.W. Bernard, *The King's Reformation*, published by Yale 2005)

There is overwhelming evidence for the king's close involvement in religious matters; for Henry's leading role in debates over the nature of true religion, in copious annotations in his own hand on various statements of faith, in his letters arguing with leading churchmen.

The evidence indicates that there were both religious and political motives for the changes introduced to the Church. The key motivation would appear to be the development of the Royal Supremacy; this spanned both politics and religion and was never modified. The emphasis on the teaching and enforcement of the Royal Supremacy was a central feature from the moment of its introduction in 1534, regardless of whether Henry seemed more inclined to radical or conservative doctrine.

Examiners' notes

Study Source 20. The skill in using this source is in drawing out the implications in the evidence. The commentary on Henry's involvement in religious debates suggests that Church reform did not take place without his sanction; thus Henry was not a disinterested party who, having obtained his annulment, left the direction of religious policy to others.

Examiners' notes

These pages give you an opportunity to review key developments in royal authority during Henry's reign. There is a lot of information summarised here. In order to use it effectively in an answer, you will need to have developed the precise knowledge outlined in previous chapters to support your arguments effectively.

Essential notes

In 1509, Thomas More was gushing in his praise of Henry when he acceded to the throne. As the young Henry was crowned, More claimed, 'This day is the end of our slavery, the fount of our liberty, the end of our sadness, the beginning of joy'.

The extent and nature of royal power

In 1509, Henry VIII had ascended the throne to general acclaim and an anticipation of great things to come. In the very early years, the king had been under the restraint and influence of his father's old councillors, Warham and Fox. As Henry matured, his reign witnessed some of the most significant developments in royal power since the early Middle Ages.

The portraits on this page depict Henry at the start and end of the period of study. Physically, he had undergone many changes; he was no longer the 'Prince Charming' described by Thomas More at the start of the reign. Age and physical infirmity brought on by a jousting accident in 1536 led to his weight ballooning and prevented him from pursing the sporting activities that had preoccupied the early decades of his reign.

The consequence was that Henry was more involved in politics than he had ever been when Wolsey led the government.

Henry VIII, anonymous portrait, 1509

Henry VIII, Hans Holbein portrait, 1540

Henry's authority as king

The rights and powers of the English monarch had been significantly extended during Henry's reign:

- The Royal Supremacy gave the king absolute authority over all his subjects, both laity and clergy.

- The increased use of statute law had confirmed its place as the supreme form of law in England. Statute law in turn named the king Supreme Head of the Church in England and enforced his position by means of the Act of Succession and the Treason Act.

- The acquisition of wealth from the monasteries offered the possibility of making the king financially independent of parliament; he would never again be thwarted in his foreign policy because of parliament's reluctance to grant his taxes.

- Henry had removed opposition to the Royal Supremacy and the English Reformation via ruthless punishments.

- He had extended his authority over the whole realm, including Wales and the north, which were notoriously difficult regions to control.

- He had produced the male heir necessary to secure the succession.

- He had removed his chief minister whose policy and methods appeared to clash with his own.

Henry's control of the Church

Undoubtedly the most significant development of Henry's reign was the establishment of an English Church entirely under his control:

- Papal authority over the clergy and the laity was removed by the Acts in Restraint of Appeals and the Act of Supremacy.

- Henry assumed responsibility for the spiritual welfare of his subjects.

- He retained the title 'Defender of the Faith', but this now applied to the reformed faith.

- He dissolved the monasteries and removed the abbots from the House of Lords.

- The faith of the English Church was defined in the Act of Six Articles.

- He applied the heresy laws to both Catholics and Protestants who defied his religious policy.

The position of the nobility: the factions

The period after 1540 is often regarded as one in which factional struggle dominated and the king was manipulated by his subjects.

Factions were always a feature of Tudor government and there is clear evidence of their effects by 1540:

- Gardiner had played a key role in drawing up the Act of Six Articles in 1539.

- The conservative faction led by Norfolk schemed tirelessly to remove Cromwell from power by 1540 and succeeded in June of that year.

- Catherine Howard, Norfolk's niece, became Henry's fifth wife on 28 July 1540.

This evidence is often used to show that the conservative faction had achieved the ascendancy by 1540.

Essential notes

Henry VIII burned 81 heretics at the stake in his 38-year reign. These included both Protestants who rejected orthodox Catholicism as well as Catholics who opposed the Royal Supremacy and the doctrine of the new English Church.

Continued on the next two pages

Compare the opinions expressed in the two sources below. They initially appear contradictory, with Scarisbrick claiming that Henry was manipulated by the factions and Schofield describing him as master of the situation. This demonstrates one of the key challenges in studying history – how is it possible for two historians studying the same sources to reach such contrasting conclusions?

Reconciling the differences is an essential skill to master in order to achieve the higher levels in the exam. So, while Scarisbrick blames the factions, he also acknowledges that the king's approval had to be achieved; this is not dissimilar from Schofield's view that the king knowingly pushed the blame onto the factions. The importance of the king is therefore a common theme in both sources.

J.J. Scarisbrick emphasises the significance of factional struggle in Cromwell's fall:

Source 21
(From J.J. Scarisbrick, *Henry VIII*, published by Eyre Methuen 1965)

He was hustled out from below, the victim of a conspiracy waged by Norfolk, aided by Gardiner and his fellows, who used Catherine Howard as their pawn. At the time, probably, Henry had never fully understood how and why Cromwell was suddenly swept away. The king had been stampeded by a faction bent on a coup d'état and swept along by it like the suggestible man that he was.

However, this argument overlooks the following evidence:

- Catherine Howard was not skilled politically and offered very little advantage to the conservatives in their attempts to influence Henry.
- Reformers such as Cranmer remained in leading positions.
- The death of Cromwell led to an increased role for the Privy Council in government, but this was balanced between conservatives and reformists and therefore did not allow conservative domination.

John Schofield argues that the downfall of Cromwell was not the primary responsibility of the conservatives. In this argument, Henry was the master of the factions not at their mercy:

Source 22
(From John Schofield, *The Rise and Fall of Thomas Cromwell*, published by The History Press 2011)

It was convenient for Henry to put all the blame on Cromwell's foes, though not especially convincing. Even the wily Winchester [Stephen Gardiner, the Bishop of Winchester] for all his craft and artifices could never have touched a hair of Cromwell's head without Henry's sanction. It was the king himself who had used Gardiner and his faction to strike "his most faithful servant" down.

Examiners' notes

The sources used here raise an important point about the necessity of knowing the details of an event and being able to place the source extracts in context. In this case, the focus is on the role of factions in the downfall of Cromwell. It is essential to know not only who was involved (which is given in the sources), but to be able to use your knowledge to explain what motivated the factions and why Henry encouraged the attacks on his chief minister. Refresh your knowledge by referring again to the events examined on pages 36–37 and 74–75.

Conclusion

The position of the king had changed by 1540.

- As shown earlier, his control over the realm had been significantly enhanced by the removal of papal authority and the establishment of the Royal Supremacy.

- His new wealth offered the possibility of establishing an absolutist monarchy that was financially independent of parliament, and his use of the Treason Act ensured that his subjects submitted to his control.

- The continued development of factions within the court could be seen as a challenge to his authority, but even here, they could not succeed in their designs without the approval of the king. It is possible to assess how far royal authority was strengthened by the end of Henry's reign.

It is possible to assess how far royal authority was strengthened in the period 1509–40.

Strengthened	Not strengthened
The Royal Supremacy gave Henry absolute power over the Church and removed any foreign interference from his realm.	The removal of Cromwell in 1540 left Henry more exposed to factional intrigue than he had been previously.
The birth of Prince Edward in 1537 secured the succession and avoided the prospect of civil war.	Henry's declining health meant that by 1540, he was not always able to attend the sessions of the Privy Council as he might desire.
The loyalty of his people was demonstrated by the limited resistance to his policies.	The wealth from the dissolved monasteries was not used wisely with significant rewards going to members of the nobility to the expense of Henry's treasury.
Henry's ruthless application of the Treason Act ensured that opposition was muted.	Henry's kingdom was no larger than it had been in 1509.
The financial position of the monarchy was significantly strengthened by the wealth from the dissolved monasteries.	
The system developed by Thomas Cromwell extended Henry's powers more effectively over Wales and the North.	
His foreign policy had been largely successful and by 1540 he was certainly the third-ranking power in Europe.	

Overall it is possible to argue that royal authority had been significantly extended by 1540; not only geographically in terms of the king's ability to enforce his will across the realm but also in its very nature: the assumption of the royal supremacy gave Henry more extensive powers than any previous English monarch had ever possessed.

Introduction

This section of the book covers the skills you must use to gain a high mark, as well as the relationship between different skills. Examples are given to illustrate various skills at different levels, although for the greatest success you should use this along with the student answers and the commentaries that show these in action (see pages 106–125).

The structure of the exam

The key similarity between (a) questions and (b) questions is that the sources will be at the centre of your answer.

There are, however, a number of differences between the way you need to approach answering (a) questions and (b) questions:

Question (a)	Question (b)
You are required to analyse and evaluate source material in relation to an issue (AO2a) – see pages 92–93.	You are required to reach a judgement about a claim or a view (AO1 and AO2b) – see pages 95–97.
You will use only contemporary sources.	You will be using a mixture of contemporary sources and secondary sources.
You use only the sources.	You use the sources and your own knowledge.

Timing

You have 1 hour 20 minutes for the whole exam in Unit 2. As the exam is worth 60 marks in total, this means spending around 25–30 minutes on question (a), including time for studying the sources, planning, writing and checking the answer. This will leave 50–55 minutes for question (b).

As with any extended answer, planning before you write is important. Although you will probably only spend around 25 minutes in total answering question (a) in the exam, time spent before this carefully studying the sources and the question is very likely to improve your focus, and the structure and quality of your answer. This doesn't mean having to do a written plan, but it is commonly found with good answers.

There are a variety of ways successful students plan for an answer:

- You could draw a simple table that sets out the basic positions of the sources in relation to the question, as show in the table on page 89.

- You could use a linear or even triangular diagram to indicate areas of agreement and disagreement between all three sources, for example as shown below.

- You could underline or highlight the different views in the sources themselves, for example using two different colours and with arrows and annotations between these to highlight potential comparisons.

However you do this, before you begin to write, you should have clearly established the position of the sources in relation to the question.

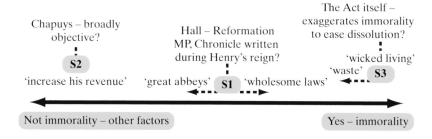

Example plan for question (a): How far do these sources suggest that it was the immorality within the smaller monasteries that accounts for their dissolution in 1536?

Answering question (a)

The (a) question is worth 20 marks and requires you to reach a judgement on the extent to which a set of sources agree or disagree on a view given in the question. The main skill you are focusing on is comparing and contrasting the evidence from the sources in relation to the issue in the question. This means:

- identifying issues where the sources relate to each other and examining the level of agreement or disagreement between them

- considering relevant aspects of the attribution, such as the purpose, origins and nature of the source, and taking account of these when you develop your comparisons.

All of these issues are examined in more detail, with examples, below.

How do you work out the focus of the question?

The golden rule here is read the question very carefully. Any time spent doing this is not wasted, as it will enable you to write a focused answer.

There are really two main issues to look for when working out the focus of question (a):

- What exactly is the issue you are expected to compare and contrast the sources over?

- How exactly is the question asking you to structure these comparisons?

Firstly, consider the language used in the question as a starting point (see page 97).

Now consider the following examples.

> **Example 1**
> *Study Sources 1, 2 and 3.*
> *How far do these sources suggest that it was the immorality within the smaller monasteries that accounts for their dissolution in 1536?*
> *Explain your answer, using the evidence of Sources 1, 2 and 3. [20 marks]*

Example 1 is on the topic of the dissolution of the smaller monasteries. However, if you study the question carefully, you can see that it asks *how far* it was the immorality within the smaller monasteries that brought about the dissolution. Therefore, the question is asking you to examine *how far* the sources show the dissolution happened *because of* immorality. This might mean identifying how important immorality or other factors are as a cause within the sources.

> **Example 2**
> Study Sources 1, 2 and 3.
> How far do Sources 1 and 2 support the view of Source 3 that Cardinal Wolsey was widely disliked?
> Explain your answer, using the evidence of Sources 1, 2 and 3. [20 marks]

Likewise, for Example 2, the topic is about Cardinal Wolsey being disliked. Here, you need to be careful to ensure that any comparisons you make are focused on the question of 'was Wolsey widely disliked?' rather than being just about Wolsey generally. In other words, you are looking to examine the sources to find *how far* Wolsey was *disliked*.

While (a) questions are always on the skills of comparing, contrasting and developing cross-references, how exactly each question is phrased varies. So, for example:

Inferencing means drawing logical conclusions and deducing what is implied by a source. It is a useful skill, as for higher marks, answers need to treat the sources as evidence. This means doing more than treating them as face value sources of information. It requires you to 'read between the lines' and work out the meaning of sources beyond what is directly stated. It may be that by inferencing, you identify how a source that mainly points in one direction also suggests or hints in another direction. A word of caution: any inference has to be a conclusion that could logically be drawn from the evidence of the source.

- Example 2 asks you to compare two of the sources – Sources 1 and 2 – against another, Source 3. On questions such as this, the source you are being asked to compare against is like an 'anchor' source. The general view of the 'anchor' source is that given in the question ('was Wolsey widely disliked?') and your points should always come back to comparing against this. Sometimes, such questions can be phrased along the lines of, 'How far do Sources 1 and 2...challenge the view of Source 3?'

- Example 1 doesn't give you a particular source to compare the others against. However, the chances are that the view given in the question ('it was the immorality...') will be closely held by one of the sources. Therefore, one way of tackling the question is by identifying this source and mainly comparing the other views to it.

One other point to bear in mind is the use of the word 'suggest' in the question. This is a handy reminder that you aren't just taking the sources at face value – you are working out from the evidence, making inferences and using other skills to consider the meaning of the evidence.

How do you cross-reference effectively?
Cross-referencing means making direct connections between two or more sources by identifying and examining areas of agreement and disagreement between them, with reference to specific examples from the sources. As a part of this process, it is vital that you use brief quotations to support your examination of the agreement or disagreement between the sources. (For example, see how this is done in the table on page 89.)

Many students start their main points with a paragraph or more on how the sources broadly agree with each other over the question, and then follow this with separate paragraphs examining ways in which they disagree. If you take this approach, you should aim to examine the extent of agreement in each section. Paragraphs that simply list examples of agreement or disagreement can tend to look a little black and white and are unlikely to achieve a level 3 or above for AO2a. It is also important that you try to see the agreement (or disagreement) in each paragraph as a starting point, going on to examine how far they agree through each point you make. Even in planning, you can try to emphasise this.

Alternatively, you could aim to structure your points more on an issue by issue manner, as in an essay. This can be very effective, although again, the golden rule should be focusing on the question and examining how far the sources do or do not agree.

Reading contemporary sources with an understanding of their nuances

This is really about being careful to study the meaning of sources to pick up on the subtle things as well as the obvious. Practice, understanding of the period the source is from, and consideration of the provenance of the source are always helpful with this. Consider Example 3:

Example 3

In February [1536] the Parliament met at Westminster, which made many good and wholesome laws. One of these gave to the King, with the consent of the great and fat abbeys, all religious houses of the value of £200 and under, in the hope that their great monasteries would still continue. But even at that time one speaker said in the Parliament House, that these were like little thorns, but the great abbeys were like rotten old oaks and they must follow.

At face value, this source tells us the larger monasteries supported the king and Reformation Parliament in passing the law to close the smaller monasteries. However, using our own knowledge of events, particularly how the monasteries were pressured by Cromwell and other representatives of the king, we can interpret this as the larger monasteries 'consenting' to the closure of the smaller monasteries as a way of protecting themselves.

Placing sources in context

While marks are not explicitly awarded for your own knowledge, you are expected to be able to place the sources in context. You should aim to use what you know to briefly consider any relevant aspects of the attribution, such as the views of the authors, to test the strength of the inferences you make and to explain your comparisons. However, keep this to a minimum, as no matter how impressive any detail you give about the issue in the question, it will not be given credit and you risk drifting from the question.

Let's consider the following example. The student is commenting on Source 2 on page 106:

Example 4

Source 2 presents the strongest evidence to counter these claims, suggesting that the dissolution was motivated by concerns other than ending immorality in the smaller monasteries. While a representative of the Spanish Emperor would be likely to be against the closures, Chapuys's letter is matter-of-fact in tone and merely refers to how 'the King will greatly increase his revenue', suggesting a financial motive.

Here the student shows understanding of the context. They demonstrate awareness that Charles V was an opponent of the Reformation, while avoiding being drawn into a detailed description of European diplomacy in the 1530s. Additionally, the answer highlights how the evidence of the source does not completely reflect the expected viewpoint, and in this sense can be seen to be stronger as evidence.

How do you 'unpack' the sources?

Unpacking the sources means taking them apart to identify the different issues they cover and the points they make. When you are practised at this, it is something you will be able to do as you read. In the exam, many students separate out the points by underlining, highlighting or annotating issues from the sources (see Examples 5 and 6 below). As you do this for one source, it is useful to consider how it relates to the other sources.

In the two examples below, the student has started to unpack their meaning by identifying points that agree and disagree with the question:

- The student has underlined and highlighted points in the source that support the view that Wolsey was disliked (Anne's own views about Wolsey and where and why he is disliked by the nobility).

- The student has used blue highlighting to distinguish points in the source that counter the argument, i.e. suggest that Wolsey wasn't disliked.

Example 5

(From George Cavendish's *Life of Wolsey*, written between 1554 and 1558. Cavendish was Wolsey's Gentleman Usher.)

I heard it reported by them that waited on the King at dinner that Mistress Anne Boleyn was much offended with the King, as far as she dared, because he made my lord [Wolsey] so welcome. 'Sir' she said, 'consider what debt and danger he has brought you into,' meaning by this the loan that the Cardinal recently tried to raise for the King from his subjects. 'If my Lord of Norfolk, of Suffolk, or my lord my father had done the same, they would have lost their heads'. *'Why then', replied the King, 'I see you are no friend of the Cardinal'.*

Example 6
(From Polydore Vergil's *History of the English*, published in 1534, after Wolsey's fall. Wolsey and Henry VIII at first supported his work, but in 1515 Vergil criticised them in a letter to the Pope and was briefly imprisoned on Wolsey's orders.)

Wolsey's abundance of fortune, in becoming the Bishop of Lincoln, the Archbishop of York, and then Lord Chancellor of England, must be seen as worthy if it befalls men who are sober, modest, and temperate, who do not boast of their power, nor become arrogant in their wealth and do not put on airs due to their good fortune. None of these things was true of Wolsey, who beginning almost immediately became so arrogant that he imagining himself the equal of sovereigns.

An alternative approach would be to identify key issues from the sources, for example how attitudes towards Wolsey depended upon his actions towards people. This could be compared with his actions towards people in Source 1 (justice for the poor) and his boastfulness and arrogance in Source 3.

A table such as that shown below helps you to see the issues raised by the sources.

Source 3	Widely disliked due to arrogance, putting on airs	
	'Peerage and commons alike'	
	Vergil's motives and time of writing	
	Supports – widely disliked	**Challenges – not disliked**
Source 1		Just, favours the poor
		'Of great repute'
		Objective, but how well informed?
Source 2	Animosity of Anne, etc.	King's support
	Cavendish doesn't deny this	'As far as she dared'

Table plan for 20-mark question, 'How far do Sources 1 and 2 support the view of Source 3 that Cardinal Wolsey was widely disliked?' (The sources for this question are found on page 111.)

How do you use the attribution?

For higher levels, answers need to treat the sources as evidence. This means doing more than treating them simply as face value sources of information. In part, this means 'reading between the lines' by working out the meaning of sources.

In addition, you need take account of relevant issues raised by the source attribution (the caption that explains the provenance of the source). These are summarised in the spider diagram overleaf.

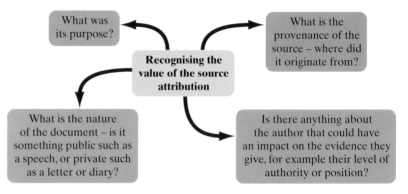

What was its purpose?

What is the provenance of the source – where did it originate from?

Recognising the value of the source attribution

What is the nature of the document – is it something public such as a speech, or private such as a letter or diary?

Is there anything about the author that could have an impact on the evidence they give, for example their level of authority or position?

Using the source attribution: key questions

The answers to the questions shown in the spider diagram have an impact on what is said in the actual source. However, for question (a) you need to be able to focus this analysis towards the question. This might mean:

- considering how the provenance of the source helps explain why it takes a different view on the issue. So, explaining why one source disagrees with another because of issues such as the political or religious views of the author

- examining how the nature or purpose of the source adds weight to (or indeed takes away from) the quality of evidence when considering how far one source supports another, as this student has done below.

Example 7
...Source 3's portrayal of Wolsey as arrogant has to be seen in the light of Vergil's personal motivations against Wolsey. Similarly, the reported words of Anne agree in so far as they suggest the nobility perceived Wolsey to be gaining special treatment. However, that Cavendish, Wolsey's loyal servant, reports this does indicate there is substance to Vergil's claims, even if only how the nobility view Wolsey. Therefore, Cavendish's evidence does strongly support this aspect of Vergil's claim, with an admittance of resentment among some at court from someone whose honesty can be expected over this.

How do you integrate attribution and cross-referencing?
Exam questions will always have something interesting within the attribution (that means, for most if not all of the sources, you have something to use). Remember, to access the higher levels you need to treat the sources as evidence. Don't just compare what they say (content) – you need to examine and infer from the meaning of what they say when making comparisons.

You should also take account of the nature, origins and purpose of the sources. Don't write paragraphs about the source content then separate paragraphs about nature, origin and purpose. Such answers usually end up talking about reliability rather than answering the question. What you should aim to do is link issues about the provenance to the points of comparison you have made. For example, the contrasting views of two differing sources may be partly explained by the different origins or purpose of the sources.

Consider the following example:

Example 8
(From George Cavendish's *Life of Wolsey*, written between 1554 and 1558. Cavendish was Wolsey's Gentleman Usher.)

This is a typical example of an attribution of a source. These should be treated like the source, and read carefully. As with the source content, many students find it useful to underline, highlight or annotate them. However, be careful of writing about the provenance for the sake of it – only make points that you can link to the comparisons you are making.

So, merely commenting that Cavendish 'was there' or that 'as Wolsey's close servant he would be biased' will gain you little credit. However, if you can link the attribution to what Cavendish says, and use it to explain why he takes a different view from one of the other sources, you will be demonstrating skill worthy of level 3 or above for AO2a.

In this example, you could say that Cavendish admits Wolsey was disliked despite his close support of him, so in this respect his evidence isn't what you'd expect and is arguably stronger for it. However, the point Cavendish is trying to make appears to be more about showing how Wolsey was popular with the king. This explains why Cavendish gives evidence that both supports and challenges the view of Vergil.

Reaching a developed judgement

If you structure your answer so that you focus on points that are broadly in agreement and then points that are broadly in disagreement, you need to make sure you examine the grey areas – the bits in-between. This might mean introducing a final point that examines the grey areas, or an extended conclusion that weights up how far they agree.

Good answers often try to reach judgement as they go along. This means more than just sticking sentences at the end of each paragraph to say whether sources agree or not. Along with the emphasis on 'how far' as you develop your points, try to give judgements that show the reasoning for your decision.

A strong conclusion always helps. This should weigh up how far the sources agree or disagree and return fully to the question. The best conclusions often weigh up the points and judgements that have been made through the answer. While you don't want to repeat what you have said, you might refer back to key issues about the evidence or views in the sources.

Key tips for structuring your answer

✓ Aim to write an answer that fully focuses on the issue in the question. Even though this is a 'cross-referencing' question rather than an essay, your comparisons need to be relevant.

✓ You don't need a lengthy introduction. Many students very briefly outline the views of the three sources then begin their main points of comparison. Others begin by briefly outlining the view of the 'anchor' source – the one closest to the view in the question – then go straight into comparing and contrasting the other sources to it. Whichever approach you take, don't start by describing the sources at length.

✓ Don't write lengthy paragraphs on individual sources. Answers that describe each source in turn may look at relevant points linked to the question, but they do not compare the sources to each other.

✓ Try to use all three sources as much as possible. This should mean that some paragraphs take a structure of 'Sources 1 and 2 mainly agree, while Source 3 takes a very different view'.

✓ Good answers will use appropriate language to help explain and structure their points.

✓ An answer that is able to emphasise and make distinctions between 'some agreement' and 'strong agreement' is more likely to address overall 'how far' the sources agree or disagree.

How will you be marked?

The AOs are the assessment objectives that you are marked on for each question. For question (a), this is AO2a – the analysis of contemporary sources. Specifically, this means examining and cross-referencing contemporary sources (from the period of history you are studying).

What does the mark scheme mean?

For question (a), there is a single mark scheme with four levels. Understanding the key differences between the levels will help you achieve a higher grade.

Read the summary of the levels below and look at the examples in the question and answers section, on pages 106–125.

Level	AO2a level descriptor	What the level means	Possible targets to reach the next level
Level 1	Comprehends the surface features of the sources and selects material relevant to the question. Responses are direct quotations or paraphrases from one or more of the sources.	Level 1 answers do not focus on the question. The answer may describe the source or quote from it, but they do not make comparisons.	Target to reach level 2: • Structure points around direct comparisons between two or more sources.
Level 2	Comprehends the sources and selects from them in order to identify their similarities and/or differences in relation to the question posed. There may be one developed comparison, but most comparisons will be undeveloped or unsupported with material from the sources. Sources will be used in the form of a summary of their information. The source provenance may be noted, without application of its implications to the source content.	Level 2 answers will point out similarities and differences in how the sources relate to the question, but the comparisons between the sources will be limited – they point out how the sources agree/ disagree, but do not examine this. If level 2 answers mention the nature, origins or purpose of the source, it is unlikely to link to comparisons of what the sources say.	Targets to reach level 3: • Develop comparisons to make sure they fully examine how far the sources agree or disagree on that point. • See the source as evidence – don't just accept it at face value. Try to consider how information the source gives is affected by its provenance when making the comparisons.
Level 3	Focuses cross-referencing on the task set. Responses will offer detailed comparisons of similarities/differences and agreements/disagreements that are supported by evidence drawn from the sources. Sources are used as evidence with some consideration of their attributes, such as the nature, origins or purpose, with some consideration of how this can affect the weight given to the evidence. In addressing 'how far' there is a clear attempt to use the sources in combination, but this may be imbalanced in terms of the issues addressed or in terms of the use of the sources.	Level 3 answers will be well-focused, making and developing comparisons. There will be some examination of how far the sources agree, including examining the connections between evidence in different sources. When the nature, origins or purpose of the sources is considered, this will be linked to the different views given in the evidence. The answer may still look at some of the sources or issues in less depth than other points.	Targets to reach level 4: • Make clear and explained judgements, e.g. about how far the sources agree/ disagree. • In your comparisons, try to weigh the evidence, consider what it says in the light of its provenance, taking this into account when making a judgement.
Level 4	Reaches a judgement in relation to the issue posed by the question supported by careful examination of the evidence of the sources. The sources are cross-referenced and the elements of challenge and corroboration are analysed. The issues raised by the process of comparison are used to address the specific enquiry. The attributes of the source are taken into account in order to establish what weight they will bear in relation to the specific enquiry. In addressing 'how far', the sources are used in combination.	Level 4 will build on level 3 skills. There will be a sufficient range of points and depth of analysis to reach a judgement of how far the sources agree, on individual points and overall. For range, there is no correct 'number' of points, but a level 4 answer will be balanced in looking at the different sources and areas of agreement and disagreement. Purpose, origins and nature is used to 'weigh up' how far the evidence supports the question.	

Answering question (b)

In the (b) question, you will select one question from a choice of two titles. Each question will be accompanied by three sources. One source will always be a contemporary source, one will always be a secondary source and the third source could be either. Within the sources there will always be at least two different points of view or two conflicting explanations.

The best approach to making your choice between the two titles is to read the questions first. If you have a clear preference, then skim read the three sources before you commit fully, so that you can check that you understand the sources. If you have no clear preference, then read the sources for each question carefully and make your choice based on the set of sources you can work most effectively with. It is really important that you fully understand the main arguments presented in the sources.

You should have left yourself about 50–55 minutes to complete this question, so you can spend 5 minutes making sure that you have made the right choice of question.

Once you have selected your question, it is very important that you spend some time planning your answer. One of the elements required to gain levels 3 and 4 for AO1 is to link your own knowledge to what is in the sources. This is almost impossible to do successfully unless you have planned your answer. Make sure that you leave enough time to do this, and that you think carefully about the main issues.

How do you work out the focus of the question?

Question (b) requires you to explore an historical view or claim and will usually begin 'Do you agree with the view that...?' The type of claim that you will be asked to assess will vary, and you should be aware of the target of the claim. Is the question asking you to weigh up the consequences or the causes of an event, or perhaps asking you to consider the significance of a person or campaign? You may also be asked to consider how far something changed.

Target	Possible key words in the question
Consequence – the impact of an event; what it brought about or changed.	'the result of'; 'the impact of' 'The question may also contain phrases indicating an impact, such as 'improved'; 'damaged'; 'increased'
Significance – the importance of a person, event or factor in influencing a particular outcome	'made an effective contribution'; 'was chiefly responsible for'
Causation – why a particular event has taken place	'the main reason'; 'the key factor'
Change and continuity – the extent to which things have altered or stayed the same	'major change to'; 'little alteration'

This is a particularly common style of question in this option:

Example 9
Do you agree with the view that, in the years 1515–25, Henry VIII and Wolsey conducted an effective foreign policy?
Explain your answer using Sources 1, 2 and 3 and your own knowledge.
[40 marks]

When answering this question, you would be expected to look at the arguments and evidence that support the view that the foreign policy of Henry and Wolsey was effective, and the arguments and evidence that suggest that it was not. So, the target of the question is to examine a judgement about the consequences of Henry and Wolsey's foreign policy. You will be using a combination of the sources and your own knowledge when you write, to enable you to reach a clear judgement that shows whether you agree or disagree with the view in the question.

Generally, planning your answer in the form of a table is an effective approach. You may feel that writing as much detail at the top of the table as there is in this example is an unnecessary waste of your time. However, it will help keep you focused on your question. For example:

Evidence that supports the view that the foreign policy of Henry and Wolsey was effective	Evidence that disagrees with the view that the foreign policy of Henry and Wolsey was effective, including other reasons why the Reformation took place

If you prefer, you could plan your answer using a continuum such as the one shown overleaf:

| The foreign policy of Henry and Wolsey was very ineffective | | The foreign policy of Henry and Wolsey was very effective |

Using a continuum to plan your essay

Another style of question might ask you to assess the significance of a stated factor in a causal question. For example:

Example 10
Do you agree with the view that the main cause of the English Reformation was Henry's belief that his marriage contravened divine law? Explain your answer using Sources 1, 2 and 3 and your own knowledge.
[40 marks]

In this case, you would be expected to begin by looking at the arguments and evidence that support the view that Henry's beliefs concerning his marriage contravening divine law was the main reason why the English Reformation took place. On the counter side, you could certainly look at the arguments and evidence that suggest Henry's beliefs over his marriage contravening divine law were not the most important cause. However, this will probably lead you to realise that there were other reasons why the English Reformation took place, and you can include these in your answer. You should use this approach to help you reach a clear judgement that shows whether you agree or disagree with the view in the question.

For this type of question, you can still plan using the table format, but you should note that the second column also needs to consider other factors behind the Reformation.

Evidence that supports the view that Henry's beliefs concerning his marriage contravening divine law was the main reason why the English Reformation took place	Evidence that disagrees with the view that Henry's beliefs concerning his marriage contravening divine law was the main reason why the English Reformation took place

If you look at the extract from Rogerson, Ellsmore and Hudson (Example 11), you will see an example of what is meant by a nuanced point. If you can identify these points where they exist, it will help you to access the higher levels for AO2b. This is not an easy skill to develop, but try practising it whenever you read. Think about what the writer is implying.

Reading and unpacking the secondary sources

There will be at least one, and possibly two, secondary sources in each question. When you read the sources, you should highlight and annotate them so that you use them as fully as you can.

You can and should read the sources at face value – that is, recognise what is clearly stated in them. There will, however, also be more nuanced points made in some (but not all) secondary sources.

In order to help you understand better how to go about reading and unpacking secondary sources, look at the two secondary sources (Examples 11 and 12) that accompany the question 'Do you agree with the view that the main cause of the English Reformation was Henry's belief that his marriage contravened divine law?', and which are examined in detail on page 120.

Example 11

(From D. Rogerson, S. Ellsmore and D. Hudson, *The Early Tudors*, published by Hodder Education 2001)

There was undoubtedly a mood in the country for changes to the Church on some level. Hostility to Churchmen was widespread and often bitter and it seems certain that Henry was at least influenced by this. It created an environment in which a break from the power of the Pope was at least conceivable. He was also influenced by Anne Boleyn's acquaintance with a group of reformist writers, including Tyndale, whose ideas clearly suited his purposes. In addition, she was in regular contact with a group of Cambridge academics, most prominently Thomas Cranmer, who confirmed Henry in his view that he was well within his rights to reject the authority of the Pope in what was a domestic affair. The seeds of the concept of Royal Supremacy are there for all to see.

It is not unusual to find a source such as this one from Rogerson, Ellsmore and Hudson, which can be used to both support the argument and to disagree with it. This source can be used at face value to challenge the view given in the question. You would certainly be credited for making use of and developing and explaining these references within your argument.

Disagreement with the view in the question could be developed using the direct references to both anti-clericalism and the influence of reformist ideas, using these points from the source (Example 11):

- 'There was undoubtedly a mood in the country for changes to the Church on some level'.

- The influence of 'reformist writers, including Tyndale' and 'Cambridge academics, most prominently, Thomas Cranmer'.

However, it is important to go beyond consideration of what the source states to see what it implies. This is what is meant by seeing the nuances in a source. For example:

- 'Seems certain that Henry was at least influenced by this' is a more nuanced and subtle argument, highlighting the nature of the connection between Henry and other factors – the mood of hostility towards the Church. The 'at least influenced by this' part of the argument indicates there is scope for analysis of the nature of this connection – what form the influence took – and how far this played a part in Henry's actions.

- 'Whose ideas clearly suited his purposes' suggests Henry had his own aims and motives. This could support consideration of the extent to which these aims concerned the legality of his marriage, his need for an heir and his desire for Anne. These issues are interlinked.

- Similarly, it was Cranmer who 'confirmed Henry in his view that he was well within his rights to reject the authority of the Pope in what was a domestic affair'. This suggests more strongly that Henry's own motives came first. Again, the precise nature of these motives would be open to your analysis, bringing in own knowledge or information from the other sources.

- Furthermore, the source suggests that it was the influence of 'Anne's acquaintance' with reformers such as Cranmer that brought their ideas to Henry's attention adds another potential angle concerning the relationship between different factors.

An answer that explicitly examines the relationship between different factors (such as 'While anti-clericalism and reformist ideas were significant, these were given prominence because of Henry's own views, confirming his own beliefs…'), will gain higher marks for AO2b. A response such as this will have demonstrated a stronger understanding of the argument of the source than one that simply lifts the relevant quotes and weaves them into the answer. Additionally, such an answer is likely to achieve a high mark for AO1, offering clear analysis which doesn't just explain the different factors, but examines the relationship between them and their relative importance.

Now read the source in Example 12 and think about how it relates to the question focus. Does it support the argument or disagree with it?

Example 12
(From G. W. Bernard, *The King's Reformation*, published 2005 Yale)

Henry's stand was potentially radical from the start: the logic that would produce the break with Rome was already there. As early as 1527 the king had come to the conclusion that his marriage contravened a divine law from which the pope could not dispense. This was not then, a policy only adopted after the failure of the legatine trial in 1529, let alone only after the rise of Thomas Cromwell from 1530. This undermines suggestions that Henry did not know what to do until someone else, whether Cromwell or Edward Foxe, later told him.

This source can be used to offer support to the view given in the question:

- 'Henry's stand was potentially radical from the start: the logic that would produce the break with Rome was already there'.

- 'The king had come to the conclusion that his marriage contravened a divine law from which the pope could not dispense'.

The source also explicitly challenges arguments to the contrary, denying that the Reformation was 'a policy only adopted after the failure of the legatine trial in 1529, let alone only after the rise of Thomas Cromwell from 1530'. It also introduces the notion that 'Henry did not know what to do until someone else…later told him'.

As well as at least one secondary source, there will also be at least one contemporary source. You should think about unpacking this in the same way as you unpacked contemporary sources in Section A (see page 88).

Integrating and cross-referencing secondary and contemporary sources

It is really important that you do not simply work through your sources one by one in sequence. This type of answer is unlikely to achieve more than level 2 in either of the assessment objectives.

You should try to treat the sources as a set which are to be used together. You will find that there are points of disagreement between the views held by the sources, but you are also likely to find points of agreement. Where possible, you should cross-reference these points, using the skills you have developed in question (a) (see pages 86–87).

Bernard argues that 'Henry's stand was potentially radical from the start', and that 'as early as 1527 the king had come to the conclusion that his marriage contravened a divine law from which the pope could not dispense'. This view about what lay behind the Reformation can be examined in the light of what Rogerson, Ellsmore and Hudson state, considering the extent to which it was a case of Henry being 'confirmed... in his view' or being 'influenced by this' anti-clericalism.

To help you understand how to go about the task of integrating secondary and contemporary sources, examine this contemporary source on Henry's marriage. This should be used together with the two secondary sources examined above (Examples 11 and 12).

As well as finding points of agreement and disagreement in the secondary sources, you can also look for these in the contemporary sources. Look at Henry's speech (Example 13) and compare what it has to say to what the secondary sources have argued.

> **Example 13**
> (Part of Henry's speech to the Lord Mayor and Aldermen of London, 8 November 1528)
>
> If it be adjudged by the law of God that she is my lawful wife, there was never thing more pleasant nor more acceptable to me in my life. But if it be determined by judgement that our marriage was against God's law and clearly void, then I shall not more bemoan my unfortunate chance that I have so long lived in adultery to God's great displeasure, and have no true heir of my body to inherit this realm.

A simple point of connection between Bernard (the secondary source) and Henry's speech (the contemporary source) is Henry's concern for the judgement over his marriage and whether it 'was against God's law and clearly void'. Henry's willingness to accept the judgement shows – if accepted at face value – that Henry is concerned with the status of his marriage in divine law. Thus, an analysis of the point can be developed using the contemporary source to examine and support Bernard's argument. However, Henry's reference to 'no true heir' also highlights how the issue of divine law has to be seen in the context of Henry's desire to secure succession.

These are related but distinct religious and political issues, which could be examined in a variety of ways using the sources. For example, you could relate the issue of succession back to Bernard's argument, and use this comparison to assess how far Henry's coming 'to a conclusion' over his marriage was down to religious arguments over his marriage, political concerns over producing an heir, or indeed the potential political gains to be made from breaking with Rome. This process demonstrates how you can move from an understanding that is located in levels 1 and 2 to an understanding that moves you to levels 3 and 4.

The most obvious point of contrast between Rogerson, Ellsmore and Hudson (Example 11) and the contemporary source is that Henry appears willing to fully submit to the Church, and so implicitly accepts the authority of Rome over the case. When looking at contemporary sources in particular, it is worthwhile studying the tone. Henry's speech reflects none of the 'mood in the country' that the secondary source reveals. In developing your analysis of the sources, you could consider the extent to which there are indeed two distinct issues, with hostility towards the Church being more about clerical abuses than a rejection of papal authority. Answers that are able to identify issues such as this and to argue about which view was the most convincing would be clearly moving into level 4.

> Remember, each set of sources brings its own issues and challenges, so you need to be prepared to apply the approach that is most suited to the particular group of sources with which you are working.

The role of attribution in question (b)

AO2b does not require that you evaluate the sources, although you will have done this in question (a). You should not comment on the attribution of the secondary sources as you are evaluating the claims that they make and their arguments. However, it may sometimes be useful to evaluate the contemporary source, if by doing so you can add weight to the arguments that you are presenting.

For example, if you consider the source in Example 13 above, an assessment of the attribution would help you to understand the tone of the piece. Henry VIII was speaking in 1528 to the Lord Mayor and Aldermen of London. While the exact purpose of his speech is not stated, valid comment could be made about the extent to which Henry wished to create a certain public image. The date may also be crucial, particularly in a question where the timing of Henry's actions and attitude to the Church is at the heart of the debate in the secondary sources. The key thing is that you clearly link what you say to your argument. Don't make a stand-alone general comment such as, 'The source is useful as it is from Henry VIII himself', as this doesn't add anything to your argument.

The role of own knowledge

Although the sources will drive your argument, you need to include relevant, specific and detailed own knowledge to support the line of argument. You may use your own knowledge in combination with the sources in one of two ways:

- You could pick up on Bernard's point (Example 12) about Henry having come to 'the conclusion' over his marriage 'as early 1527' and use it to discuss the extent to which Henry's views were determined by other developments from this point onwards, such as the attempt to gain a papal annulment and indeed the Pope's own changing circumstances in the light of Charles V's occupation of Rome.

- Alternatively, you could develop Rogerson, Ellsmore and Hudson's point about Anne's connection to reformist writers by discussing her influence over Henry (Example 11) and weighing this against the influence the reformers had more directly via Cromwell and Cranmer from 1529 onwards.

Make sure that when you are using your own knowledge to develop what is in the source(s), that you link the points clearly together in the same section of your answer. The easiest way to make sure that you do this is to add your own knowledge to your plan when you have finished studying the sources. You could use a different colour so you can see what is from the sources and what is from your own knowledge.

You could also make an entirely new point that has not been dealt with in the sources. Sometimes, the sources may only cover part of the time span laid down in the question, in which case you could use your own knowledge to ensure you cover the whole period.

Reaching a developed judgement

Bear in mind that you are weighing up a claim or a view and that you will have at least two alternative points of view. You need to think carefully about whether you agree with the claim made in the question or not. Try to argue your case throughout the essay, explaining why you agree or disagree with the arguments that you are presenting.

Although you should aim to make judgements throughout your answer, it is also important that you pull them together in a substantial conclusion. There are different approaches to writing a conclusion, but one possible approach would be to identify the main lines of argument that you have considered in the answer, making it clear which one you feel to be the most convincing and why. Make sure that you leave enough time for the conclusion and ensure that you include references to the sources in your conclusion, do not simply repeat what you have said in the essay and do not write a conclusion which is not in line with your argument in the essay.

Key tips for structuring your answer

Do

✓ Write an answer which focuses on the question throughout.

✓ Approach your introduction by stating which sources support the claim and which disagree with it.

✓ Make sure when referencing the sources that you number them correctly.

✓ Begin by examining the evidence that supports the claim that is made in the question.

Remember, you are not evaluating the sources but rather the claims they are making, using your own knowledge to support any judgements that you make. There is no 'right' answer to any question; the examiner will be looking at the quality of your arguments and the way you use the sources and your own knowledge to support them.

✓ Try to draw out the nuanced points in the sources and cross-reference them wherever you can.

✓ Make sure that the sources are fully integrated with your own knowledge.

✓ Use appropriate language to help explain and structure your points.

✓ Include a substantial conclusion in which you clearly reach a judgement about the extent to which you agree or disagree with the claim made in the question.

Don't

✓ Work through the sources in sequence.

✓ Work through own knowledge in a separate section.

✓ Evaluate the secondary sources in terms of their nature and origins.

✓ Ignore the issues in the presented sources.

✓ Use abbreviations that are not common practice, e.g. POG rather than Pilgrimage of Grace.

What does the mark scheme mean?

As question (b) involves two assessment objectives, it requires you to demonstrate a number of skills. This means you need to be really aware of the requirements of the question and how the mark scheme works.

The Assessment Objectives

- The purpose of Assessment Objective 1 (AO1) is to assess your ability to recall historical knowledge and use it in conjunction with the sources to address the focus of the question.

- The purpose of Assessment Objective 2b (AO2b) is to assess your ability to analyse and evaluate judgements about the past. This is not the same as you are asked to do in the question (a), as you are not necessarily expected to deal with the attribution of the sources.

Level	AO1 level descriptor	AO1 – What the level means	AO1 – Possible targets to reach the next level
Level 1	Produces mostly simple statements. These will be supported by limited factual material which has some accuracy and relevance, although not directed at the focus of the question. The material will be mostly generalised. There will be few, if any, links between the simple statements. The writing may have limited coherence but will be generally comprehensible, but passages will lack both clarity and organisation. The skills needed to produce effective writing will not normally be present. Frequent syntactical and/or spelling errors are likely to be present.	Level 1 answers will take a descriptive approach to the question that is very generalised and has very little specific information about the topic.	Target to reach level 2: • Look at the description and make some links between it and the question.

Level	AO1 level descriptor	AO1 – What the level means	AO1 – Possible targets to reach the next level
Level 2	Produces a series of simple statements supported by some accurate and relevant factual material. The analytical focus will be mostly implicit and there are likely to be only limited links between the simple statements. Material is unlikely to be developed very far. The writing will have some coherence and will be generally comprehensible, but passages will lack both clarity and organisation. Some of the skills needed to produce effective writing will be present. Frequent syntactical and/or spelling errors are likely to be present.	Level 2 answers will take a descriptive approach to the question, but will be based on more detailed knowledge and make some links to the question, although these will only appear occasionally in the answer.	Targets to reach level 3: • Focus directly on the question so that you are able to attempt some analysis by looking at arguments that both agree and disagree with the claim in the question. • Plan your answer. This will help you to integrate the sources with your own knowledge of the topic.
Level 3	Attempts analysis and shows some understanding of the focus of the question. They will, however, include material which is either descriptive, and thus only implicitly relevant to the question's focus, or which strays from that focus. Factual material will mostly be accurate but it may lack depth and/or reference to the given factor. The writing will be coherent in places but there are likely to be passages which lack clarity and/or proper organisation. Only some of the skills needed to produce convincing extended writing are likely to be present. Syntactical and/or spelling errors are likely to be present.	Level 3 answers will be aware of the question focus. They will look at the arguments that support the claim in the question and those that disagree with the claim. Both the sources and some specific and detailed own knowledge will be used at times in the answer, and there will be some links made between these, although these are likely to be only occasional.	Targets to reach level 4: • Draw out in more detail the conclusions that you reach about the view in the question, based on the sources and your own knowledge. • Integrate the sources and your own knowledge. • Show a detailed knowledge base of the issues raised in the question.
Level 4	Offers an analytical response which relates well to the focus of the question and which shows some understanding of the key issues contained in it. The analysis will be supported by accurate factual material which will be mostly relevant to the question asked. The selection of material may lack balance in places. The answer will show some degree of direction and control but these attributes may not be sustained throughout the answer. The candidate will demonstrate the skills needed to produce convincing extended writing but there may be passages which lack clarity or coherence. The answer is likely to include some syntactical and/or spelling errors.	Level 4 answers will approach the answer in a similar way to level 3, but will develop the arguments more extensively throughout the answer. They will integrate the sources with own knowledge more frequently, and the quality of the supporting evidence from the student's own knowledge will be very strong.	

Level	AO2b level descriptor	AO2b – What the level means	AO2b – Possible targets to reach the next level
Level 1	Comprehends the sources and selects material relevant to the representation contained in the question. Responses are direct quotations or paraphrases from one or more of the sources.	Level 1 answers will generally contain a few brief quotations lifted from the sources, which have not always been understood. They are very likely to work through the sources in sequence.	Target to reach level 2: • Make sure that the sources have been used to provide evidence of both agreement and disagreement with the view in the question.
Level 2	Comprehends the sources and selects from them in order to identify points which support or differ from the representation contained in the question. When supporting the decision made in relation to the question, the sources will be used in the form of a summary of their information.	Level 2 answers will generally use the sources more extensively and points will be picked out from them that agree or disagree with the view presented in the question. They are still likely to be summarising what the sources say. They may work through the sources in sequence.	Targets to reach level 3: • Write an introduction which identifies the different arguments that are to be found in the sources. • Use the different arguments identified as the basis for the answer which has been planned out. This will help you to approach the answer analytically rather than working through the sources in sequence.
Level 3	The sources are analysed and points of challenge and/or support for the representation contained in the question are developed from the provided material. In addressing the specific enquiry, there is clear awareness that a representation is under discussion and there is evidence of reasoning from the evidence of both sources, although there may be some lack of balance. The response reaches a judgement in relation to the claim which is supported by the evidence of the sources.	Level 3 answers will show an understanding that the sources clearly present differing interpretations in relation to the view expressed in the question. This is likely to be achieved by examining the evidence that agrees with the view in the question and then looking at the evidence that disagrees with it.	Targets to reach level 4: • Read the sources carefully so that you can establish not just the arguments that they present at face value, but so that you can also draw out the inferences and deal with these in your answer. • Evaluate the arguments in the sources on the basis of what the other sources say and your own knowledge of the events.

Level	AO2b level descriptor	AO2b – What the level means	AO2b – Possible targets to reach the next level
Level 4	Reaches and sustains a conclusion based on the discriminating use of the evidence. Discussion of the claim in the question follows from the issues raised by the process of analysing the representation in the sources. There is developed reasoning and weighing of the evidence in order to create a judgement in relation to the stated claim.	Level 4 answers will draw out all the key issues from the sources and evaluate whether or not they agree with the arguments by judging them against the other sources and the student's own knowledge.	

Exemplar essays and commentaries

Unit 2, Question a (i)

Study Sources 1, 2 and 3.

How far do these sources suggest that it was the immorality within the smaller monasteries that accounts for their dissolution in 1536?

Explain your answer, using the evidence of Sources 1, 2 and 3.
[20 marks]

Source 1

(From Edward Hall's *Chronicle, a history of the early Tudors* published 1542. Hall was a London lawyer and MP in the Reformation Parliament.)

In February [1536] the Parliament met at Westminster, which made many good and wholesome laws. One of these gave to the King, with the consent of the great and fat abbeys, all religious houses of the value of £200 and under, in the hope that their great monasteries would still continue. But even at that time one speaker said in the Parliament House, that these were like little thorns, but the great abbeys were like rotten old oaks and they must follow.

Source 2

(From a letter written by Eustace Chapuys, the Imperial Ambassador, to Charles V of Spain, 18th March 1536)

It has been determined in Parliament that the monasteries not worth more than £200 annual rent shall be suppressed, by which the King will greatly increase his revenue. He has also proposed to Parliament a law that every one shall be bound to give offerings, to be collected by men deputed by the King, in order therewith to feed the poor. The King has also determined that only parish priests should hear confessions. The priests are to be ordered not to absolve anyone who does not hold the Pope for Antichrist, and the King for head of the Church.

Source 3

(From the Act of 1536 dissolving monasteries with an income of less than £200 a year)

Manifest sin, vicious, carnal and abominable living is being daily used and committed among the small abbeys, priories and other religious houses. The governors of such religious houses spoil, destroy, consume and utterly waste their properties to the high displeasure of almighty God. And although many continual visitations have been made for an honest and charitable reformation, yet their wicked living shamelessly increases, so that unless such small houses are utterly suppressed there can be no reform of these matters.

For Unit 2, question (a), you are required to analyse and evaluate source material in relation to an issue.

This question requires you to consider the extent to which each source suggests that immorality within the smaller monasteries was the main cause of the dissolution of 1536. You will need to consider what each source indicates about the reasons for the dissolution, bearing in mind the provenance of the source. A good answer will make direct and focused comparisons between all three sources in relation to the question.

Grade C student answer

Source 3, the Act of Dissolution itself, most strongly suggests that immorality within the smaller monasteries led to their dissolution. The Act offers a solid case against the monasteries, describing in shocking terms a range of activities that could be seen as immoral. This suggests that while attempts have been made in order to bring about a 'charitable reformation' of these, the 'manifest sin' and other acts of immorality continues and even 'shamelessly increases'.

Source 1 supports this to some extent. Hall states that that the Act dissolving the monasteries was a 'good and wholesome' law, and this appears to support the view that the closure of the smaller monasteries was necessary due to immorality. While Hall's account lacks detail in this respect, the reference to 'little thorns' could be taken to mean that the lesser monasteries were a source of corruption. However, this is somewhat ambiguous. Being linked to the issue of the 'rotten old oaks' of the great abbeys could point to immorality within both, with the difference being one of scale. However, it may also suggest that the dissolution of the smaller monasteries was simply part of a process leading to the closure of the great abbeys, with thorns more in the sense of barriers to Henry's overall plans. So, Source 3 appears to offer stronger evidence that the dissolution was a result of immorality.

Source 2 presents the strongest evidence that the dissolution was motivated more by concerns other than ending immorality in the smaller monasteries. Chapuys refers to how 'the King will greatly increase his revenue', suggesting a financial motive. This is to some extent supported by Source 1's reference to giving 'to the King', with both recognising that aside from any other motives, Henry stood to gain from the dissolution financially. So, while Source 3, which only refers to resources in terms of how the monasteries 'waste their properties', acknowledges the financial issue, Sources 1 and 2 identify more clearly how Henry stood to profit from dissolution.

Additionally, Source 2 suggests another motive of Henry's – ensuring support for the break with Rome. Chapuys reports the instruction to priests to only give absolution to those who accept the break with Rome. This suggests that many of the suppressed monasteries had continued to give spiritual comfort, and even encouragement, to those who continued to ☞

Here the student outlines how the view of Source 3 relates to the issue in the question. This can be a valid approach, particularly for outlining the view of the source that is closest to the view given in the question. It is also useful when the question does not specify the 'anchor' source. The key advice here is to stay focused: avoid describing the view of any source at length, as the primary focus needs to be cross-referencing the different views. To raise the level of this part of the response the student would need to briefly summarise how the views of the other sources relate to the view of Source 3.

Here the student demonstrates a good understanding of Source 1 and examines in depth how this relates to the view in the question. However, while the student compares the evidence to the question, the comparison to the other sources is brief and largely implicit, with no real cross-referencing of views. For this reason, the answer remains at level 2 for AO2a.

This paragraph makes direct comparisons between all three sources, with some cross-referencing of the detail. This is worthy of a level 3 response for AO2a, but lacks the depth of development to reach level 4. Also, there is no real consideration of the provenance of the sources, with only passing reference to Chapuys.

support the Pope's position. This could be linked to Source 1 to some degree, seeing the collective measures as a way of ending such behaviour among the smaller monasteries while also serving as a warning to the great abbeys over what would happen if they did not back Henry. Along with this, Source 2 clearly indicates that Henry sought to ensure that spiritual and other forms of relief continued after the closures. This does not in itself confirm the 'wicked living' of Source 3. It does, however, indicate a desire to provide for the spiritual well-being of the population, suggesting the reforms may in part have been motivated by the failings over this that the Act details.

The final paragraph fulfils the criteria for level 3 at AO2a – it again shows a strong grasp of both the issue and the viewpoints taken by the sources. There is direct comparison between sources, developing and examining the extent of agreement between Sources 1 and 2, and then relating this to the view of Source 3. This shows an overall awareness of how far the sources are in agreement. However, the answer is not fully developed. A more clearly structured point, expanding on this, would improve the answer.

There is a strong overall focus on the issues, and the student develops comparisons relating to the question, considering both how the sources agree and disagree with the view in the question. There is some cross-referencing of the detail from the sources to make valid points. However, there would need to be more detailed cross-referencing to achieve a level 4 for AO2a.

Additionally, while there is some recognition of the sources as being evidence beyond face value, such as reasoned inferencing and implicit consideration of their purpose and context, this is not explicitly considered. To improve to level 4 for AO2a, the student needs to fully and directly consider the purpose, origins and nature of the sources and the impact this has on the given evidence.

The answer could also further examine 'how far' the sources agree. Currently, there is limited judgement and no overall conclusion. In part this is because of the structure of the answer, which largely deals with the sources on an individual basis. To improve this response, the student needs to make more direct and focused comparisons between all three sources in relation to the question.

Overall, this answer achieves a **low level 3 for AO2a, and would gain 12 marks.**

Excellent Grade A student answer

Of the three sources, it is Source 3, the Act of Dissolution itself, which most strongly suggests that immorality within the smaller monasteries led to their dissolution. It describes in shocking terms a range of activities that could be seen as immoral. Source 1 supports the reasons given in the Act (Source 3) to some degree. Hall, a member of the Reformation Parliament, states that that the Act dissolving the monasteries was a 'good and wholesome' law, and this appears to support the view that the closure of the smaller ☞

The answer begins with a very clear focus on the question, identifying and examining Source 3 as that which most closely relates to the view in the question. This is followed by direct cross-referencing with Source 1, which analyses the extent to which the two sources agree.

monasteries was necessary because of the immorality within them. While Hall's account lacks detail on this aspect, the reference to 'little thorns' could be taken to mean that the lesser monasteries were a source of corruption, so agreeing with the picture of 'manifest sin' and the increase in 'wicked living' that Source 3 portrays. Being linked to the issue of the 'rotten old oaks' of the great abbeys may suggest the problem of immorality within both, with the difference being one of scale. However, Hall seems more to imply that the dissolution of the smaller monasteries was part of a process leading to the closure of the great abbeys, so 'thorns' in this sense may mean barriers to Henry's overall plans. While Hall's tone appears supportive of the closures, he appears to admit that if anything, the problems were worse in the 'rotten old oaks' of the greater abbeys. This could suggest other motives. So, while Source 3 clearly details the corruption and lack of morality, this can be seen as justifying what was convenient; immorality may have existed in many of both the lesser and greater houses, but the smaller ones were closed first as this was easier. The Act may overstate the problems to justify the closure, yet it is Hall's evidence that states the 'great and fat abbeys' consented to allow the smaller ones to be sacrificed to save their own positions. Therefore, while Source 3 appears to offer the strongest evidence that the dissolution was a result of immorality, the source must ultimately be seen as a product of Henry's Parliament.

Source 2 presents the strongest evidence to counter these claims, suggesting that the dissolution was motivated by concerns other than ending immorality in the smaller monasteries. While a representative of the Spanish Emperor would be likely to be against the closures, Chapuys's letter is matter-of-fact in tone and merely refers to how 'the King will greatly increase his revenue', suggesting a financial motive. This is to some extent supported by Hall's more pro-Reformation views in Source 1, with reference to giving 'to the King'. That both of these are written once the closures have begun may suggest that the financial gain was an added benefit to Henry rather than the prime motive for closure. Nevertheless, even Source 3 refers to how the monasteries 'waste their properties', and the fact is that Henry stood to profit from dissolution, so immorality alone cannot fully account for this. ☞

The latter part of this first paragraph continues to develop an in-depth comparison between Sources 1 and 3, which is well focused on the question. The origins, purpose and tone of the sources are considered in examining how far the evidence from the two sources is in agreement, with clear and reasoned judgement given.

This answer also demonstrates a sophisticated writing style. The student has a very clear grasp of the question and the position of the source texts in relation to it, and so is able to write an extended paragraph exploring the comparison between Sources 1 and 3. An answer could gain equally high marks by breaking this paragraph down into shorter, more structured points.

In this paragraph, the student considers the evidence of Source 2. The position of the source in relation to the question is quickly identified, while the student acknowledges the provenance of the sources, and this supports a focused and direct comparison of all three. All three sources are used in combination in the process of reaching a judgement relating to the question. To improve even further, the points linking these back to Source 3 could be examined in greater depth.

Additionally, Source 2 suggests that another motive of Henry's was to ensure support for the break with Rome. Chapuys's reporting of instruction to priests only to give absolution to those who accept the break with Rome suggests that many of the suppressed monasteries had continued to give spiritual comfort, and perhaps even encouragement, to those who continued in their loyalty to the Pope. Source I can be seen to support this analysis to some degree, in that the collective measures are viewed as a way of ending rogue behaviour among the smaller monasteries while also serving as a warning to the great abbeys of what would happen if they were not loyal to Henry. It is no surprise that the issue of submitting to Henry's supremacy is only openly acknowledged in the Imperial Ambassador's report. Hall's was a pro-Reformer writing after the event who was still mindful of Henry's approval, and he focuses more on how Parliament solved the problems within the monasteries. Similarly, in Source 3, while the reference to 'the high displeasure of almighty God' may refer to control of the Church, this is not a matter the Act has any reason to draw attention to. In this way, Source 2 highlights broader motivations for the reform of the Church that cannot be denied, but which the other sources play down.

Therefore, the evidence must be seen to suggest that while immorality did exist in the lesser monasteries, this fact made a convenient excuse to extend Henry's control over the Church while allowing him to gaining financially from the disssolution. In this sense, Chapuys, despite his Imperial leanings, offers a more balanced explanation of why the smaller monasteries were closed. The shameful behaviour detailed in the Act itself has to be seen to some extent as the justification by Henry's Parliament. While this behaviour may have been found in some cases, Hall's evidence, although similarly limited by his position, suggests more of a planned programme that Chapuys seems to confirm.

Here, the answer develops an in-depth comparison between Sources 1 and 2, effectively cross-referencing their views over support for Henry. Again, the attributes of the sources are carefully examined in considering the position they take on the issue. Source 3 is then brought into the comparison, with a tentative judgement that emphasises how far the sources agree. This demonstrates the skills required to achieve a level 4 for AO2a.

The answer reaches a conclusion that offers a clear judgement on the question. This relates the views of all three sources to the overall conclusion, considering the position they take in the light of their provenance. This clearly gives weight to the evidence, and while relatively brief, is clearly linked to the analysis of preceding paragraphs. Although the answer achieves a level 4 for AO2a, it could be improved by examining the relative weight given to the sources further.

There is very good overall focus on the issues. Points are well developed, offering a thorough and appropriately balanced consideration of the issues. Cross-referencing of detail is used to help analyse the views of the sources in relation to each other. Attribution is considered, and issues such as the provenance of the sources are clearly applied to the examination of the differing views of the sources. The answer clearly examines 'how far' the sources agree, with developed points exploring the extent of agreement, both through the answer and in the conclusion.

Overall, this response is worthy of a **high-level 4 for AO2a, and would gain the full 20 marks.**

Unit 2, Question a (ii)

Study Sources 1, 2 and 3.

How far do Sources 1 and 2 support the view of Source 3 that Cardinal Wolsey was widely disliked?

Explain your answer, using the evidence of Sources 1, 2 and 3.
[20 marks]

Source 1

(From a report written by the Venetian ambassador to England in 1519, sent to the Venetian government.)

The Cardinal [Wolsey] has a reputation for being extremely just. He favours the people exceedingly, and especially the poor, hearing their cases and seeking to deal with them immediately. He is of great repute – seven times more than if he were Pope.

Source 2

(From George Cavendish's *Life of Wolsey*, written between 1554 and 1558. Cavendish was Wolsey's Gentleman Usher.)

I heard it reported by them that waited on the King at dinner that Mistress Anne Boleyn was much offended with the King, as far as she dared, because he made my lord [Wolsey] so welcome. 'Sir' she said, 'consider what debt and danger he has brought you into', meaning by this the loan that the Cardinal recently tried to raise for the King from his subjects. 'If my Lord of Norfolk, of Suffolk, or my lord my father had done the same, they would have lost their heads'. 'Why then', replied the King, 'I see you are no friend of the Cardinal'.

Source 3

(From Polydore Vergil's *History of the English*, published in 1534, after Wolsey's fall. Wolsey and Henry VIII at first supported his work, but in 1515 Vergil criticised them in a letter to the Pope and was briefly imprisoned on Wolsey's orders.)

Wolsey's abundance of fortune, in becoming the Bishop of Lincoln, the Archbishop of York. And then Lord Chancellor of England, must be seen as worthy if it befalls men who are sober, modest, and temperate, who do not boast of their power, nor become arrogant in their wealth and do not put on airs due to their good fortune. None of these things was true of Wolsey, who beginning almost immediately became so arrogant that he imagining himself the equal of sovereigns. Thus by his insolence and ambition Wolsey sought and earned the dislike of the entire people, since he was hated by Peerage and Commons alike.

This question requires you to consider the extent to which each source suggests that Wolsey was unpopular. You will need to consider what each source indicates about Wolsey's popularity, bearing in mind the provenance of the source. A good answer will make direct and focused comparisons between all three sources in relation to the question.

Grade C student answer

Source 3 clearly states that Cardinal Wolsey 'earned the dislike of the entire people'. Polydore Vergil sees this as being largely a result of Wolsey's arrogance, flaunting his wealth and status. Source 2 suggests some agreement with this; Anne's complaint with Wolsey may be directly regarding the consequences of the failed loan, although her tone and Henry's response that he saw she was 'no friend of the Cardinal' indicate clear dislike. While on the face of it the sources appear to broadly agree on the extent to which Wolsey was disliked but not the motives, Anne's comment that Wolsey was treated favourably compared with Norfolk suggests a resentment and jealousy that is in agreement with the view of Vergil in Source 3. Of the two sources, Source 2 is more reliable, as while Cavendish would be expected to favour Wolsey, being his long-standing servant and biographer, he admits the resentment of Anne and the nobles. In contrast, Vergil has the motive to speak against Wolsey, having been imprisoned by him, and also the opportunity to settle scores, writing freely after Wolsey had died while being out of the King's favour.

While Source 2 reveals a strong dislike of Wolsey, Source 3 claims that this feeling was not widespread. In Source 2, the dislike is from a section of the nobility, with no indication of the 'Commons alike', as Vergil states. While this aspect is not mentioned in Source 2, Source 1 directly challenges this view. The Venetian ambassador reports how Wolsey is of great repute, seemingly as a result of the work he does in giving justice to the 'people…especially the poor'. In this way, Source 1 challenges Vergil's view in Source 3. This suggests that resentment over Wolsey's superiority, his wealth and his putting 'on airs' was confined to the 'Peerage', while the ordinary people of England respected Wolsey for the swift and fair treatment they received through the courts.

While Source 3 is blunt on how Wolsey was widely hated, it does show that the dislike grew alongside Wolsey's increasing status and boastfulness. This helps explain the differences between the sources. Source 1 is positive towards the Cardinal and is from early on in his reign, before such resentment had grown. Source 2 shows Anne and the nobility were against Wolsey, although at this point he still had the King's support. Source 3 is written after Wolsey's fall from power.

A valid comparison is made between Sources 2 and 3, and there is an initial examination of how far the sources agree. The student also recognises the need to consider the provenance of the sources. Unfortunately, the analysis is not directed towards answering the question, but looks at and compares the reliability of the sources. For this reason, this part of the answer would achieve no higher than level 2 for AO2a.

Here, the student gives a focused and direct comparison which brings in all three sources. Such direct and focused comparisons are often typical of answers at level 3 or above for AO2a, particularly if all three sources are used. In addition, the structure of the comparison is good and the origins of the evidence are recognised.

To improve further, the paragraph could explore the extent of agreement and disagreement between Sources 1 and 3. Similarly, the student could consider relevant points concerning the provenance of the sources to examine why they offer differing viewpoints on Wolsey. Without this, the evidence from the sources is accepted at face value. This lack of consideration of the attributes of the sources limits the paragraph.

Here, the student makes direct comparisons and contrasts between the sources. There is some recognition of the importance of provenance in explaining each source, for example the importance of the date of each source is acknowledged. Yet, the comparisons are not fully explored.

Making effective use of the provenance of the sources is a skill that some students find difficult. Compare this paragraph with the first one on the Grade A student answer, to see the difference in how it is done.

There is a clear focus on the issue under discussion and the comparison of sources. There is some cross-referencing of detail, although this lacks the depth necessary to achieve a level 4 for AO2a. The answer is also rather limited in the range of points made. For example, while the student considers the purpose, origins and nature of the evidence, the first attempt to consider attribution regarding the provenance of Sources 2 and 3 is little more than a comparison of reliability that adds little to developing an examination of the evidence. While the latter assessment of the chronology of the sources is more in tune with the demands of the question and demonstrates sound understanding, it again lacks depth. To raise this answer to a level 4 for AO2a, the source comparison needs to be fully used to answer the question about Wolsey's popularity.

Overall, this answer would achieve a **low level 3 for AO2a, gaining 12 marks.**

Grade A student answer

Source 3 clearly states that Cardinal Wolsey 'earned the dislike of the entire people'. Polydore Vergil sees this as being largely a result of Wolsey's arrogance, flaunting his wealth and status. As may be expected, Anne Boleyn's complaint within Source 2 implies some agreement with this. Although Anne's offence may be a result of the failed loan, her tone and Henry's response that he saw she was 'no friend of the Cardinal' indicate clear dislike. Sources 2 and 3 appear to broadly agree on the extent to which Wolsey was disliked, but suggest different motives. Anne's comment that Wolsey was treated favourably compared with Norfolk or others would appear to suggest resentment and jealousy, and this is in agreement with the view of Vergil in Source 3. In this sense, the evidence does suggest Wolsey was disliked. Cavendish, from whom loyalty may be expected, suggests Anne took against the Cardinal, which agrees with the view of Vergil, who would be expected to be more critical of Wolsey having been imprisoned by him. Vergil's view may also reflect the fact that he is writing after Wolsey's fall and death, giving him licence to extend his emnity to the 'dislike of the entire people'.

It could be argued that while Source 2 reveals strong dislike of Wolsey, this was not widespread as Source 3 claims. In Source 2, the dislike is from a section of the nobility, with no indication of the 'Commons alike', as Vergil states. While this aspect is merely unmentioned in Source 2, Source 1 directly challenges Source 3. The Venetian ambassador appears to take a more objective viewpoint, although his report is written when ☞

The paragraph makes a direct comparison between Sources 2 and 3 that is clearly focused on the question and is developed to explore the differences between the two sources and examine how far they agree. One important skill the student demonstrates here is that of going beyond merely highlighting similarities and differences.

Additionally, the student considers and applies relevant issues concerning the provenance of the sources, using this to extend the comparison. For example, the student considers the relationship of both Vergil and Cavendish to Wolsey and when they wrote. In this way, the paragraph highlights qualities of a good level 3 and potential level 4 for AO2a, considering the weight of the evidence in relation to the required comparison. To achieve a level 4 for AO2a, an answer would need to display such skills on a consistent basis.

Wolsey was still in his ascendancy. He states how Wolsey is of great repute, seemingly as a result of the work he does in giving justice to the 'people…especially the poor'. The evidence in Source 1 directly challenges the view of Vergil in Source 3, suggesting that resentment over Wolsey's superiority, his wealth and his putting 'on airs' was confined to the 'Peerage', whereas the ordinary people of England respected Wolsey for the fair treatment they received through the courts.

Therefore, Sources 1 and 2 seem to challenge the view that Wolsey was widely disliked. Source 1's more positive portrayal of the Cardinal is from early on in his reign, perhaps before such resentment had grown, but its reporting of his popularity among 'the people' has to carry some merit. Furthermore, Source 2, presumably from just after the failed Amicable Grant, suggests that Wolsey still has the faith of the King. While Source 2 indicates there was resentment towards Wolsey, this appears as strongest within certain court factions. Thus, the view of Source 3 is only partially correct, being accurate in how it reflects the attitudes of sections of the nobility towards Wolsey, but it over-exaggerates the extent to which this resentment was widespread, at least during the Cardinal's lifetime.

Again, the student puts forward a confident argument regarding the agreement and disagreement between the sources. This clearly relates the viewpoint of all three sources to the question and each other, and the evidence is cross-referenced. Similarly, the consideration of the provenance of Source 1, while relatively brief, is used effectively, and is to some extent linked to that of Source 3, although this could be examined further. While the depth of development could be improved, the student has demonstrated the skills necessary to achieving a low to mid level 4 for AO2a.

This response concludes with a clear judgement on the extent to which the three sources agree over the issue of Wolsey's popularity. The student gives weight to the evidence that the sources provide, exploring the impact of the sources' provenance on the differing positions they take and their status as evidence. These skills are necessary to achieve a level 4 for AO2a.

There is a sharp focus on both source comparisons and the issue in the question, with good cross-referencing throughout. There is considered application of source attributes, and this is used to examine the varying views of the sources. Finally, a reasoned judgement is given that attempts to give weight to the evidence.

To improve to a high level 4 for AO2a, there needs to be greater depth of development. For example, the consideration of the provenance of the sources in relation to the question could be examined more fully. Also, while there is effective cross-referencing of sources, the student missed the opportunity to examine a greater range of points.

Overall, this answer is worthy of a **lower to mid level 4 for AO2a, and would gain 17 marks.**

Unit 2, Question b (i)

Use Sources 1, 2 and 3 and your own knowledge.

Do you agree with the view that the Pilgrimage of Grace was less a result of religious grievances and more a result of social and economic motivations?

Explain your answer using Sources 1, 2 and 3 and your own knowledge.
[40 marks]

Source 1

(From Susan Brigden, *New Worlds, Lost Worlds*, published 2000 Allen Lane)

Led by Robert Aske, their Grand Captain, who was both visionary and politic, the Pilgrimage united the grievances of a whole society against alien innovations from the South, devised by heretic evil counsellors around the King. The pilgrims' grievances were inevitably economic, social and political, as well as narrowly religious, but only the defence of Holy Church, now lame and fast in bounds, could have united so many different groups in this mass demonstration and overlaid it, through long awaited days, with an almost mystical aura.

Source 2

(From the Oath of the Honourable Men, the oath taken by all those following the Pilgrimage of Grace in 1536. The Oath was devised by Robert Aske.)

In your hearts put away fear and dread, and take before you the Cross of Christ, and in your hearts His faith, the Restitution of the Church, the suppression of these Heretics and their opinions, by all the holy contents of this book.

Source 3

(From R. Lockyer and D. O'Sullivan, *Tudor Britain*, published 1997 Longman)

The Pilgrimage of Grace was a complex movement, not confined to one area and involving many social elements. The Pilgrims' Articles include a mixture of economic, political and religious grievances – high taxes, enclosure, the Statute of Uses, the loss of feast days and a range of privileges, clerical and feudal. To these can be added the cumulative effect on conservative northerners of the many sweeping changes in religion that Cromwell's government was imposing, but dislike of change was not confined to religion.

For Unit 2, question (b), you are required to reach a judgement about a claim or view using a combination of contemporary and secondary sources and your own knowledge.

This question requires you to consider the relative importance of the different factors that caused the Pilgrimage of Grace. The question proposes that the rebellion was primarily motivated by social and economic factors. You need to weigh up this view against other factors that led to the Pilgrimage, with reference both to the sources and your own knowledge.

Grade C student answer

The Pilgrimage of Grace was clearly religious as its name suggests. However, as all three sources show, there were other factors motivating those who joined the uprising.

Many of the grievances which led to the unrest were economic, social and political in nature, as Source 1 shows. As Source 3 adds, these also varied in regions that saw uprisings, as well as in the different class groups involved. The high taxes and the Statute of Uses that Source 3 mentions were both economic concerns. These were listed in the rebels' grievances at the Lincolnshire rising of October 1536. The Statute of Uses in particular upset the gentry and lower nobility, as they saw it as a limit on their ability to leave property in wills. The unpopularity of this was shown when it faced resistance in passing through Parliament in 1536. High taxes were a particular problem for the poorer groups who made up most of the pilgrims, particularly as the risings grew into Yorkshire and Lancashire later in October. So, real concerns about economic conditions were a major part in causing the Pilgrimage of Grace.

Source 3 says how the Pilgrimage was 'not confined to one area'. As stated, poverty was a particular issue in the areas of Lancashire and Yorkshire where the greater rebellions took place. Bad harvests in the years 1535 and 1536 brought many people in these areas into the rebellion. This was demonstrated in the uprising, as enclosure had led to the destruction of hedges. For many, concerns over Cromwell's reforms that Source 3 describes were more social and economic than religious. The dissolution of the smaller monasteries had closed one of the main areas of relief from poverty, as the monasteries had given alms to the poor and other support to the needy.

Social concerns also affected the higher classes involved in the Pilgrimage of Grace. 'Cromwell's government was imposing' (Source 3) changes which limited the position and powers of the lesser nobility and gentry, with 'alien innovations from the South' (Source 1). This meant that even families such as the Percys and Lord Darcy were divided or involved in the uprisings as they turned against what they saw as centralisation under Cromwell. In this way, there was clearly important social causes for the Pilgrimage.

Aske's Oath (Source 2) clearly shows that religion was a cause of the rebellions. The closure of the monasteries and other changes was a religious issue at the ☞

While this introduction shows an understanding of the question, it is very brief. A lengthy introduction is not a requirement of the 40-mark essay, but is effective in building the foundations for an analytical response and so is credited by examiners. A better introduction would outline the arguments concerning the different motivations of the Pilgrimage, and set out the nature and relative importance of religious, social and economic factors.

This paragraph considers the economic motivations behind the Pilgrimage. It is well focused and offers some level of analysis, by beginning to examine how economic concerns grew, using detail from Source 3 and own knowledge. To improve to the level for AO1, the student needs to fully explore the importance of economic concerns in actually causing the Pilgrimage, perhaps analysing which social groups were most motivated by economic factors.

Here, Source 3 is considered again. The basic analysis is sound and supported with the student's own knowledge, making it worthy of level 2 for AO2b. To improve to level 3 or above, the student needs to identify the argument in the source and examine it using their own knowledge. Source 3 reflects a particular view on events, and this needs to be further explored.

In terms of AO1, this paragraph is somewhat descriptive, lacking clear argument, and so is more indicative of level 3. The point about Cromwell's reforms being more social and economic than religious needs to be made more prominent, perhaps by starting the paragraph with an argument that links to this. In order to reach level 4, this point could be examined fully, using the evidence to help reach a judgement on the relative importance of the issues it has raised.

This paragraph focuses on the question, selecting relevant examples from both Sources 1 and 3 to explain how social (and arguably political) issues were behind the Pilgrimage. To improve this paragraph the student needs to extend the analysis by using their own knowledge and/or the other source to examine how important these changes were.

local level. All of the 30,000 men who supported Aske at the peak of the rebellion did so by taking the oath. The Pontefract Articles issued in December 1536 were mainly a set of religious demands, aiming as they did to return aspects of supremacy to the Papacy. The appeal to the 'Cross of Christ' gave the rising 'an almost mystical aura', as Source 1 states. The 'suppression of' the 'Heretics' (Source 2) and 'evil counsellors' (Source 1) also show the significance of religious issues to the Pilgrimage of Grace.

In the end, the Pilgrimage of Grace was easily dealt with. The fact that the pilgrims maintained their loyalty to King Henry suggests this wasn't mainly a political uprising. That they were peaceful also hints at the religious element. The background economic suffering took many to the point of rebellion. This was made worse by religious changes that brought suffering for some. However, it was the 'defence of the Holy Church' which united all of the rebels under the same banner, showing that religion was not less important than other factors.

In this paragraph, the view within Source 2 is effectively linked to an argument about the role religion played. This is in turn linked to the student's own knowledge and to further evidence from Sources 1 and 2. To improve the student needs to clearly examine and assess how significant the issue of religion was in relation to other factors.

There is a hint of analysis of the views within the sources in this paragraph. However, the sources are mainly used to illustrate arguments. To raise this answer to a level 4 for AO2b, there would need to be a more thorough source analysis.

The conclusion attempts to draw together different factors and does ultimately give a judgement on the importance of religion. However, not all of the factors referred to are effectively tied to the assessment given. To improve the paragraph could be more sharply focused and give a judgement that examines the relationship between the different factors mentioned, weighing up the relative importance of these. Ideally, this would also weigh up the evidence from the sources.

For AO1, the answer achieves a mid level 3 (16 marks). It is mostly focused, with an overall structure that targets the question. There is some analysis, although parts are descriptive. The answer has a fair range of coverage, although it is more limited on religion. There is some integration of sources and own knowledge, which is accurate if lacking real depth. To improve to a level 4, the student needs to extend the analysis. Own knowledge could be better used to support a more balanced assessment of social, economic and religious issues. The conclusion requires more weighing up of the various factors and analysis of the links between them.

This answer achieves a high level 2 (7 marks) for AO2b. The use of evidence is largely supportive. The sources are used frequently, and there is some integration with own knowledge. To improve to a level 3 or 4 for AO2b, the views and arguments of both the primary and secondary sources in the paragraph need to be examined critically in relation to the question.

This answer would gain **23 marks**.

Grade A student answer

While Sources 1 and 2 highlight the significance of religious grievances in bringing about the Pilgrimage of Grace, they also demonstrate that economic and social factors also played a role. Source 3 takes this further, detailing a range of other issues that were behind the uprisings of 1536.

Although this is a somewhat brief introduction, the student has demonstrated a clear grasp of the question and the position that each source takes in relation to it.

The interrelated nature of these wider factors makes it difficult to weigh the precise importance of specific causes. As Lockyer and O'Sullivan highlight in Source 3, many of the grievances which promoted unrest were economic, social and even political in nature and were varied in their significance in regional and class terms. Thus, high taxes and the Statute of Uses, both listed in the rebels' grievances at the Lincolnshire rising of October 1536, reflected the economic concerns of different groups. The former was a particular concern of poorer groups as the Pilgrimage of Grace proper spread to Yorkshire, while the latter was resented by the gentry as a feudal restraint on their ability to bequeath property in wills (this had faced resistance when passing through Parliament in 1536). Although Source 1 is perhaps correct to suggest that 'only the defence of Holy Church…could have united so many', the build up of grievances across such a range of social groups cannot be underplayed.

These social and economic issues must be seen in a geographical context. Source 3 is correct to stress how the Pilgrimage of Grace was 'not confined to one area'. As stated, poverty was a particular issue in the areas of Lancashire and Yorkshire, where the greater rebellions took place. Aske, who led the rebellion from this stage, may emphasise his own conservative religious motives in Source 2, and so serve as an example of a 'conservative northerner' in Lockyer's terms, but for the masses the hardship they were experiencing on the back of bad harvests brought them to the stage of rebellion. In areas where enclosure had taken place, the destruction of hedges demonstrated this. Equally, some of the concerns over Cromwell's reforms were really more economic. Worries over issues of tenancy, with the Crown replacing the Church as landlord, were behind fears over the dissolution, thus confirming the arguments of Source 3 over the dislike of the change Cromwell 'was imposing'. For those leading the masses, some of these concerns were more socio-political – the 'alien innovations from the South' (Brigden) points to were of real concern to the lesser nobility and gentry, who were increasingly alienated by what they saw as centralisation under Cromwell and court factions. This is shown by the involvement of Sir Thomas Percy and Lord Darcy in the rebellion.

That said, the economic and social factors must be seen in context of religion. If Aske's Oath (Source 2) is taken at face value, this was the true and direct cause ☞

The student begins the main body of the essay with a confident focus, demonstrating an understanding that a strong answer will 'weigh up' the different factors. They outline how the various factors 'worked' in differing ways to bring about the Pilgrimage of Grace, noting how they are 'interrelated'. This is effectively linked to the view of Source 3, and developed using specific knowledge to examine the different economic concerns across social groups. A link is then made to Source 1, leading to a clear judgement that both accepts and counters the given view. Such features make this a clear level 4 paragraph for AO1.

The use of sources is not quite as strong and so only merits level 3 at AO2b. To improve to level 4, the discussion and analysis of the sources needs to be fuller.

This paragraph gives a thorough, coherent and focused analysis of the relative importance of different issues, considering their significance across different geographical and social perspectives. This is clearly level 4 analysis for AO1 – the argument draws on own knowledge and all three sources in examining the issues.

The use and analysis of the sources is also high-level here, and there is effective use of the contemporary source (Source 2). The student stays firmly focused on AO2b, examining how the argument and views of the sources relate to the question. The provenance of the source is considered, though it is not discussed in any depth (as required for AO2a) but focuses more on using the source to consider the implications of Aske's evidence. The student is confident in using their own knowledge to evaluate the given evidence, with reasoned judgements given.

of the rebellions. In this sense, Brigden's argument that religious appeal was essential in binding such a varied range of groups deserves consideration. While the closure of monasteries and other changes was a religious issue at the local level, religion can be seen to be the one factor held in common by the 30,000 men who supported Aske at the peak of the rebellion. Aske may have devised the oath to suit his own demands, but this was continued in the Pontefract Articles issued in December 1536, which maintained a predominantly religious tone, and in particular aimed to return aspects of supremacy to the Papacy. In this sense, it was the appeal to the 'Cross of Christ' (Source 2) which gave the rising 'an almost mystical aura' (Source 2). That it was the 'suppression of' the 'Heretics' which was behind this, essentially targeting the likes of Cromwell and 'evil counsellors' (Source 1), fitted easily with political and other motivations and made the appeal of the oath even easier.

Therefore, while it is hard to deny that the Pilgrimage of Grace was brought about by social and economic motivations that were substantial and widespread, religious grievances were the glue that held this together. While Source 3 is correct that the rebellion was not confined to religion, with almost none of the tangible changes that had brought grievances being solely religious, Source 1 is correct to emphasise how the 'defence of the Holy Church' was the banner which united the pilgrims. Brigden may overstate this, as for many this banner cloaked deeper motives and grievances, but the notion of the rebels being Pilgrims was evident in the words and deeds of those involved.

As this question asks the student to reach a judgement concerning the relative importance of two different issues, it is important that both of these are dealt with properly. While religion has been mentioned in previous paragraphs, here the student brings balance to their answer by offering a clear and well-reasoned analysis and evaluation of the role played by religion. This is examined and weighed against other factors, and would achieve a level 4 for AO1. To improve further, the judgement could be extended to provide better coverage of AO2b by assessing the strength of the arguments from the sources mentioned.

This conclusion makes a well focused and clearly explained judgement. The significance of religious motives is clearly weighed in relation to other factors, drawing on the views of Sources 1 and 3 in reaching a conclusion. While not fully fitting with the balance of the essay, which seemed to give more consideration to factors other than religion, the judgement is well-reasoned and is confident in assessing the given representations.

For AO1, the answer achieves a high mid-level 4 (22 marks). The answer has clear focus, being structured around arguments and offering confident judgements. Accurate and specific factual material is integrated with the sources to support a consistent analysis. The answer is overall balanced, with reasoning that examines the relationship between different factors. To improve to a high level 4, the student could examine the motivations of different groups further.

For AO2b, the answer achieves a level 4 (14 marks). The student clearly identifies and analyses the representations in the given sources, confidently integrating the evidence from the sources within. The arguments in each paragraph are based on references to more than one source, and there is reasoning and weighing up of the evidence. To improve there could be a greater range in the analysis of the evidence.

Overall, this answer would gain **36 marks**.

Unit 2, Question b (ii)

Use Sources 1, 2 and 3 and your own knowledge.

Do you agree with the view that the main cause of the English Reformation was Henry's belief that his marriage contravened divine law?

Explain your answer, using Sources 1, 2 and 3 and your own knowledge.
[40 marks]

Source 1

(From D. Rogerson, S. Ellsmore and D. Hudson, *The Early Tudors*, published by Hodder Education 2001)

There was undoubtedly a mood in the country for changes to the Church on some level. Hostility to Churchmen was widespread and often bitter and it seems certain that Henry was at least influenced by this. It created an environment in which a break from the power of the Pope was at least conceivable. He was also influenced by Anne Boleyn's acquaintance with a group of reformist writers, including Tyndale, whose ideas clearly suited his purposes. In addition, she was in regular contact with a group of Cambridge academics, most prominently Thomas Cranmer, who confirmed Henry in his view that he was well within his rights to reject the authority of the Pope in what was a domestic affair. The seeds of the concept of Royal Supremacy are there for all to see.

Source 2

(From G. W. Bernard, *The King's Reformation*, published by Yale 2005)

Henry's stand was potentially radical from the start: the logic that would produce the break with Rome was already there. As early as 1527 the king had come to the conclusion that his marriage contravened a divine law from which the pope could not dispense. This was not then, a policy only adopted after the failure of the legatine trial in 1529, let alone only after the rise of Thomas Cromwell from 1530. This undermines suggestions that Henry did not know what to do until someone else, whether Cromwell or Edward Foxe, later told him.

Source 3

(Part of Henry's speech to the Lord Mayor and Aldermen of London, 8 November 1528)

If it be adjudged by the law of God that she is my lawful wife, there was never thing more pleasant nor more acceptable to me in my life. But if it be determined by judgement that our marriage was against God's law and clearly void, then I shall not more bemoan my unfortunate chance that I have so long lived in adultery to God's great displeasure, and have no true heir of my body to inherit this realm.

This question requires you to consider the relative importance of the different factors that gave rise to the English Reformation. The question proposes that Henry's beliefs concerning his marriage contravening divine law was the main reason for the Reformation. You will need to weigh this argument against other factors that led to the Reformation, both from the sources and using your own knowledge.

Grade C student answer

Henry may have believed that his marriage contravened divine law, seeing this as a reason why Catherine had failed to produce a male heir. However, there were other reasons why he began the process which led to the break from Rome, including his desire to marry Anne and the influence others who wanted to change the Church.

The argument that Henry's 'marriage contravened divine law' as the main cause of the Reformation is supported by Source 2, which claims that Henry realised this as far back as 1527. Henry had read Leviticus and was by this time increasingly influenced by what the scripture said, suggesting as it did that he and Catherine would not produce a male heir as he had uncovered 'the nakedness of his brother's wife'. Although this doesn't show that Henry planned to actually break from Rome, the king was attempting to use this passage to persuade the Pope that his marriage was invalid. However, the problem for Henry was that this challenged the Pope's authority over the original dispensation to marry, and so was effectively a challenge to Papal authority generally. However, by the time Campeggio had arrived in England in 1528, the Emperor Charles V, Catherine's nephew, had increased his influence on the Pope and so an easy annulment was less likely. In this way, the belief Henry had that his marriage contravened God's law became even more important as time went on, as increasingly the only option to annul the marriage was to break from Rome.

Source 1 shows other reasons why the Reformation began. As the source describes, England before the Reformation was ripe for change, with many people unhappy with the Church. Many saw the Catholic Church as being in poor condition, with poorly educated parish priests and wealthy monasteries that did little for the spiritual well-being of the people. Events such as the Hunne case had turned people away from the Church, while practices such as the selling of indulgences and bishops and priests holding several offices caused anger and resentment. Source 1 also shows how the influence of Lutheran ideas that disagreed with the Catholic Church were growing, with 'Cambridge academics' such as Cranmer and Foxe becoming important in Henry's case for a divorce. Tyndale's English Bible was being sold in increasing number, and although this was illegal, Henry was influenced by these ideas.

In breaking with Rome and beginning the Reformation, Henry was also influenced by Anne Boleyn. Source 1 mentions Anne's links to the reformers. Henry was ☞

The introduction demonstrates understanding of the question, highlighting the stated factor – Henry's belief concerning the validity of his marriages while also raising some other potential causes. Within a fairly brief paragraph, this sets up the rest of the response to be well focused on the question. To improve further, it could set out more clearly any key arguments relating to the factors mentioned.

Here, the answer focuses on the stated factor from the question. A clear point is made and developed from the start, using the evidence from Source 2 and specific and relevant own knowledge to examine the argument that Henry's beliefs were influential in breaking with Rome. This makes the answer worthy of a level 3 for AO1. However, not all of this detail is 'used' effectively; for example, while the student gives detail relating to the Pope being effectively hostage to Charles V by 1528, the implications of this are not explored. To improve to a level 4 for AO1, the interrelationship between these developments and Henry's actions needs to be examined.

Similarly, while the answer does in some way recognise a view given within the source, this is not clearly developed. In this way, the answer displays a level 2 skill for AO2b, as although the evidence from the source is linked to own knowledge, there is no analysis and the answer soon moves away from the source. A higher level response would have recognised the view taken by the source and used own knowledge to examine it.

This paragraph focuses on other causes of the English Reformation. There is some consideration of the question, although this is quite implicit and descriptive. The paragraph links back to the question, although the absence of clear argument and analysis means the claim that Henry was influenced by anti-Catholic sentiment is asserted and not supported. To raise the level of the response for AO1, the student would need to consistently use knowledge to analyse, rather than describe.

besotted by Anne and also believed she could provide him with the male heir he needed. Although in Source 3 he claims that he would be happy with Catherine, he had already fallen in love with Anne by 1527, so it is hard to take what he says at face value. Indeed, it is probably more that he is trying to convince the Aldermen of London that his case for divorce is based on genuine concerns over his marriage to Catherine. By this time, Henry had grown tired of Catherine.

Anne was also more likely to bear Henry the heir he needed. Henry shows this in Source 3 where he mentions God's displeasure if his marriage is seen as void. Although he talks about God's displeasure, he actually hoped for the marriage to be found as void at this time, as that would mean he could marry Anne. Although Henry had a daughter, Mary, by Catherine, he was wary that it was unlikely she would be accepted on the throne. In Henry's time, Yorkist contenders for the throne were still seen as a potential threat, so it was important for him to secure the throne with a male heir, and Henry Fitzroy, his only son to survive infancy, was illegitimate.

Overall, it can be seen that Henry's concern over the legitimacy of his reign was certainly an important reason for the beginnings of the Reformation, as it is hard to argue that Henry aimed to make the changes to the Church that Source 1 indicates. The reasons for his challenging the Pope were because of his concerns over securing his succession and his falling for Anne, as he came to see Catherine as unable to produce the heir he needed. Source 2 shows the belief that the marriage to Catherine was invalid, and although that may have been because no male heir had been born, the evidence suggests Henry was convinced of this by the late 1520s.

Here, the student considers the role played by Anne Boleyn. Both Sources 1 and 3 are referred to, being linked to some degree with the point made. The student attempts to examine the provenance of Source 3. This examination is applicable to an extent, as this is the one contemporary source of the three, and Henry's purpose does have a bearing on what he says. The student is implying that Henry's evidence here, while apparently supporting the stated claim in the question, can actually be discounted. The answer attempts to use the evidence critically, but the approach to source evaluation suits question (a) more. For level 3 or higher in AO2b, the answer would need to apply this, examining the implications of Henry's purpose and reaching a judgement focused on a point made about the claim.

Here, the student develops a point which isn't really considered in the sources, discussing Henry's desire for a male heir. The student uses their own knowledge in combination with Source 3 to link to the issue of contravening divine law through the reference to 'God's displeasure'. In this way, there is analysis worthy of level 3 for AO1. To achieve level 4, the analysis would need to be much more clearly argued and focused, with assessment of the relative significance of the different causes.

The conclusion offers a judgement and draws together some of the points examined. There is some attempt to explain the judgement, although it is not fully reasoned. The judgement also links to two of the sources and indicates an understanding of the evidence they give. To improve further, there needs to be a summary that is more clearly focused on the importance of Henry's beliefs concerning his marriage. It should also reach a judgement on the views in the sources, for example explaining which of the two sources mentioned offers the stronger argument as to why the Reformation took place.

For AO1, the answer achieves a mid level 3 (16 marks). The student attempts analysis, with some strong development in places, and at times the response offers specific and relevant knowledge. The answer usually returns to the focus of the question, with some assertion linked to own knowledge. Thus, overall, the answer is broadly analytical. To gain a higher grade, the student's own knowledge needs to be directed more fully to answering the question. The analysis needs to be more focused, with a conclusion that links clearly back to own knowledge and analysis.

For AO2b, the answer achieves a high-level 2 (7 marks). The student shows a good understanding of the sources and how they relate to the points raised. There is some integration of the sources with own knowledge. However, the sources are used to illustrate the points that are made. To improve to a level 3 or 4, there needs to be more developed analysis of the evidence.

Overall, this answer gains **23 marks**.

Grade A student answer

The English Reformation took place in the 1530s. Henry took the steps to move away from Rome because he needed a divorce from Catherine so that he could marry Anne and produce a male heir. However, although the divorce issue stemmed from the issue of the legality of Henry's marriage, there were other factors, such as the role of the anti-clericalism mentioned in Source 1, which would explain why the Reformation took place.

The brief introduction sets out a clear understanding of the question. The student identifies the way in which Henry's beliefs over his marriage affected the other factors to be examined. What makes this opening stronger than the previous example, is that it also indicates a line of argument. To improve further, the student could also outline the arguments concerning the relative importance of other factors.

As Source 2 shows, it was clear to Henry and his advisers that his 'marriage contravened a divine law'. Although his long marriage to Catherine had produced a daughter, Mary, by 1527 Henry was influenced by reading the Hebrew translation of Leviticus, which told him Catherine and he would be without sons. Henry's need to secure the Tudor dynasty with a male heir meant that he accepted the Levitical argument and pressed for a divorce on the grounds that the original dispensation was not legitimate. Source 3 suggests Henry was willing to accept the 'judgement' on his marriage. However, the failure of his marriage to Catherine to produce a male heir, with her being 42 years old, meant Henry genuinely saw potential danger for the Tudor dynasty after his death, particularly with the existence of rival claimants such as the Pole family. In this way, it is clear Henry had decided that as his marriage was illegal, he saw no other option. This started the chain of events that led to the Reformation.

Here, the student examines the stated factor from the question. A clear argument is developed in relation to the view of Source 2, using detailed knowledge and Source 3 to examine Henry's belief concerning the validity of his marriage. Although the strength of the argument is not as explicit in its analysis as some other paragraphs, words such as 'although', 'however', 'genuinely' and 'particularly' are used with effect to accentuate points. The views of the sources are clearly recognised and integrated with the analysis. To improve further, the sources could be more explicitly evaluated using knowledge or evidence from the other sources.

Additionally, Bernard (Source 2) argues that Henry knew that his marriage was invalid from the very start ☞

of the process, and understood that the Pope could not in truth have given the dispensation that enabled him to marry Catherine. The apparent willingness to accept the judgement of a legatine trial under Campeggio that Henry shows in Source 3 seems to disagree with this. Henry was still keen to produce a convincing public case to demonstrate the invalidity of his marriage. Rather than reject Papal authority to decide on the case, Henry's willingness to wait for the decision suggests he was confident of achieving a divorce with relative ease. So while the issue may have ultimately led to the Reformation, it is hard to see this as planned by Henry.

In this paragraph, the student clearly sees the sources as representations that take a particular view on events. The student identifies the view taken by Source 2 and analyses this using Source 3 and well-selected own knowledge. A confident argument is maintained through the paragraph, with a clear judgement being offered at the end.

Other factors need to considered that had an impact on the course of events and ultimately helped bring about the English Reformation. Source 1 highlights two significant other factors which are to some extent linked, which are growing anti-clericalism and the role of Anne Boleyn. The first of these is clearly evident in England by the 1520s, and Rogerson et al. are right to point to growing 'hostility to Churchmen'. However, while there may have been a 'mood in the country for changes… on some level', it is harder to evidence this as directly contributing to the English Reformation. Lutheran ideas challenging Papal infallibility were largely confined to Cambridge academics.

Again, the student is confident in identifying the argument within a source and taking an analytical approach to it, demonstrating level 4 skills for AO2b. While this analysis is not fully developed, the point is clearly reasoned. To improve even further, the student could conclude this paragraph by returning to the view of Source 1 and giving a clear judgement about the strength of its arguments.

More radical ideas could have been more influential in contributing to the Reformation through Anne Boleyn and her circle of acquaintances, as Source 1 highlights. While such ideas may have lacked popular support, as the divorce case dragged on, it was the likes of Cranmer and Foxe who proposed seeking the opinions of the European universities on this matter. While Henry may have had little enthusiasm for the Protestant ideas of such men, the opportunity to solve his problem within England that they offered was increasingly attractive. Henry may have claimed in Source 3 that he was willing to abide by God's judgement, but it is clear by 1532, when Cromwell began to initiate parliamentary legislation, that the political aspects of the Reformation were his will. That Henry was besotted by Anne through the late 1520s added to the growing impatience and thus influence that the radical groups had. So, Source 1 is correct to highlight Anne's increasing importance as the case dragged on as the link between Henry's growing frustration and those who translated this into the actions that began the legal break from Rome. ☞

Here, the student offers clear argument through the paragraph. It begins with an argument about the influence of radical ideas. One strength of this is that the changing importance over the period is examined. Knowledge and sources are again well integrated, and on this occasion, a judgement is made on Source 1's view on the question.

Therefore, while Bernard is correct to say that Henry was potentially radical in his approach as early as 1527, and he may have believed his marriage contravened divine law, at that point his preference was still for an annulment from Rome. Cromwell and others may not have 'told him' what to do, but Henry was clearly keen to seek guidance on the matter throughout the period 1527–32. Therefore, it must be seen that it was a growing frustration with the failure to resolve the Great Matter that pushed Henry towards more radical solutions. The English Reformation was only one possible means to solving his problem, and so the course of events really determined what happened. Political reformation suited Henry both in terms of solving his marriage issue and gave the added benefit of increased political authority over England, even if Henry cared less for the religious developments.

In this final paragraph, a clear and well explained decision is given on the question. This is well developed, and the relationship between a range of factors is considered in explaining an overall judgement that is well focused. This judgement is related to the views of Bernard (Source 2). This part of the conclusion offers scope for further improvement: the decision reached could be linked more fully to the views of Source 2, as well as the other sources.

For AO1, the answer achieves a mid-level 4 (21 marks). There is a clear overall focus and the argument is mainly well developed. Accurate and specific factual material is used on a consistent basis to examine points, and this is integrated with the sources, supporting and challenging the evidence they give. The answer is balanced, examining the factor that is proposed in the question alongside other factors. Additionally, it is balanced in the sense that points are examined, considering counter-arguments and the relative importance of other factors where relevant. There is also a reasoned examination of the relationship between factors, rather than just dealing with points in isolation, and connections between them are examined.

For AO2b, the answer achieves a low level 4 (13 marks). The student clearly analyses the representations in the sources, recognising the positions they take on the question and the issues they raise. The views given within them are examined and assessed, with some judgements made. However, the sources are not fully explored, with the answer leaning towards own knowledge in places. To improve further, more consistent analysis and judgement using the sources could be made.

Overall, this answer gains **36 marks**.

Page numbers in *italic* show an illustration.

Index